千年风华　山水画卷　时代新章

何以江西

2024

JIANGXI

BEFORE

JIANGXI

江西省人民政府新闻办公室　编

江西人民出版社
Jiangxi People's Publishing House
全国百佳出版社

图书在版编目（CIP）数据

何以江西 . 2024 / 江西省人民政府新闻办公室编 . --
南昌：江西人民出版社，2025. 6. -- ISBN 978-7-210
-16492-0

Ⅰ . K925.6

中国国家版本馆 CIP 数据核字第 2025MP5456 号

何以江西 2024
HEYI JIANGXI 2024

江西省人民政府新闻办公室 编

策划编辑：梁 菁 张芝雄
编辑统筹：蒲 浩 邓慧敏
责任编辑：周伟平
责任印制：潘 璐
封面设计：章 雷

江西人民出版社 出版发行
Jiangxi People's Publishing House
全国百佳出版社

地 址：江西省南昌市三经路 47 号附 1 号（邮编：330006）
网 址：www.jxpph.com
电子信箱：jxpph@tom.com
编 辑 部：0791-86898965
发 行 部：0791-86898815
承 印 厂：长沙超峰印刷有限公司

开 本：889 毫米 × 1194 毫米 1/32
印 张：7
字 数：100 千字
版 次：2025 年 6 月第 1 版
印 次：2025 年 6 月第 1 次印刷
书 号：ISBN 978-7-210-16492-0
定 价：60.00 元
赣版权登字 -01-2025-257

序 章
Prologue

山水赣鄱　魅力新篇
Ganpo Landscape　New Glowing Chapter

何以江西？

这是煌煌历史天空下，周敦颐、朱熹、陆九渊、王阳明等巨匠大儒的哲学之问。

How to Define Jiangxi?

It's a philosophical question asked by Confucian masters such as Zhou Dunyi, Zhu Xi, Lu Jiuyuan, and Wang Yangming throughout the long history of China.

何以江西？

这是滕王高阁上的王勃、庐山瀑布下的李白、醉翁之意中的欧阳修、"桃李春风一杯酒"的黄庭坚、"情不知所起，一往而深"的汤显祖，无与伦比的文学表白。

How to Define Jiangxi?

It's reflected in the unparalleled literary declaration of love made by Wang Bo (王勃) on the Pavilion of Prince Teng (Tengwangge, 滕王阁), Li Bai (李白) beneath the waterfall in Mount Lu (Lushan,庐山), Ouyang Xiu (欧阳修) in his essay The Old Drunkard's Pavilion, Huang Tingjian (黄庭坚) savoring "peach and plum blossoms in spring breeze over a cup of wine," and Tang Xianzu(汤显祖) who penned "love arises unknowingly, yet grows profoundly".

何以江西？

这是一万年稻作文明、三千年青铜文化、两千所古代书院、一千年瓷都窑火的璀璨见证。

How to Define Jiangxi?

It's a glittering witness of ten-thousand-year rice cultivation civilization, three-thousand-year bronze culture, two thousand ancient academies, and one-thousand-year porcelain kilns.

何以江西？

这是一份内涵丰盈、气势豪迈、意境深远，既充满浪漫主义悬念，又答案笃定、未来可期的宏阔答卷。

How to Define Jiangxi?

It's a resplendent tapestry woven with profound connotation and boundless vigor—a masterpiece that blends romantic enigmas with unwavering resolve, its answers etched in stone yet its horizons glowing with boundless potential, a grand testament to the ages ahead.

是的，江西古韵悠长，人文渊薮；江西绿意盎然，山青水碧；江西产兴业旺，流光溢彩；江西包容开放，心向蔚蓝；江西红根深植，万紫千红。

It is true that Jiangxi is a place where ancient melodies linger in timeless elegance with talents and civilizations converging like rivers to the sea; Jiangxi is a place where emerald landscapes cradle mountains that kiss the clouds and waters that mirror the heavens; Jiangxi is a place where prosperity thrives, industries bloom like gilded tapestries, and opportunities shimmer like molten gold; Jiangxi is a place where openness embraces the world with a heart as vast as the ocean blue; and where revolutionary spirit runs deep, nourishing a thousand hues of progress and unity.

日月经天，江河行地；东方风劲，赣鄱潮涌。

江西，这片古老又充满活力的土地，一江（赣江）一湖（鄱阳湖），谱写出山水与人文的交响；一山（井冈山）一岭（牯岭），擘画了这片土地的厚重与辉煌。

The sun and moon trace their eternal paths across the heavens; rivers and mountains carve their timeless courses through the earth. The east wind surges with invincible force, and the tides of Ganpo (Jiangxi) roar with vigor—a symphony of cosmic rhythm and earthly transformation.

Jiangxi—an ancient yet vibrant land, where River Gan(赣江) and Lake Poyang (鄱阳湖) compose a symphony of mountains and rivers combined with humanity and nature; where Jinggang Mountain(井冈山) and Ridge Guling(牯岭) etch the profound contours of a civilization's resilience and splendor.

今天的江西，历史在这里沉淀，文明在这里生长；今天的江西，执着追索，激情迸发，步履铿锵。

在新时代的伟大征程中，在4500万人民的美好憧憬里，江西，正以崭新的姿态、昂扬的斗志、坚定的决心，拥抱旷古未有的时代巨变，焕发激荡人心的澎湃力量，奋力谱写中国式现代化江西篇章。

Today, Jiangxi crystallizes history into wisdom, and blooms civilization with each new dawn; Jiangxi's relentless pursuit ignites passion, and every step resonates with the thunder of progress.

On the grand course of this new era, amid the radiant hopes of 45 million people, Jiangxi stands tall with a reborn spirit, a soaring resolve, and an unwavering will—embracing epochal transformations of unprecedented scale, unleashing a tide of electrifying momentum, and writing a radiant chapter of Chinese modernization.

对历史最好的致敬，就是抒写新的历史；对未来最好的期许，就是创造更美好的未来。

风景独好的江西，永远值得您期待！

The best respect to history is to refresh it. The best expectation to future is to create a brighter one.

Unique and picturesque Jiangxi is always worthy of your expectations.

江西位于中国东南部，长江中下游南岸，毗邻浙江、福建、广东、湖南、湖北、安徽六省，地处长三角、珠三角和闽南金三角的共同腹地，2—3小时经济圈覆盖上海、广州、厦门等主要城市。

Jiangxi is located in southeastern China along the southern bank of the middle and lower reaches of the Yangtze River, neighboring six provinces—Zhejiang, Fujian, Guangdong, Hunan, Hubei and Anhui. It serves as the shared hinterland of the Yangtze River Delta, Pearl River Delta, and Hokkien Golden Triangle, forming a two-to-three-hour economic corridor that links such major cities as Shanghai, Guangzhou, and Xiamen.

江西简称"赣"，因公元733年唐玄宗设江南西道而得省名，又因为江西最大河流为赣江而得简称。

Jiangxi (江西) derives its name from the Jiangnan Xidao(江南西道)established by Emperor Xuanzong of the Tang dynasty in 733, while its abbreviation "Gan" (赣) comes from River Gan, the largest river in Jiangxi.

江西省总面积16.69万平方公里,辖南昌、景德镇、萍乡、九江、新余、鹰潭、赣州、吉安、宜春、抚州、上饶11个设区市,100个县(市、区),其中61个县、12个县级市、27个市辖区。

Jiangxi Province covers a total area of 166,900 square kilometers and administers 11 cities with districts: Nanchang(南昌), Jingdezhen(景德镇), Pingxiang(萍乡), Jiujiang(九江), Xinyu(新余), Yingtan(鹰潭), Ganzhou(赣州), Ji'an(吉安), Yichun(宜春), Fuzhou(抚州), and Shangrao(上饶). It has 100 counties (county-level cities and districts) in total, including 61 counties, 12 county-level cities, and 27 municipal districts.

南昌，古称"豫章"，江西省省会，全省政治、经济、文化中心，辖6区3县及3个国家级开发区，总面积7195平方公里，2024年常住人口667.04万人。

Nanchang(南昌), historically known as Yuzhang(豫章), is the capital of Jiangxi Province and serves as the political, economic, and cultural hub of the whole region. Nanchang City administers six districts, three counties, and three national-level development zones, covering a total area of 7,195 square kilometers. In 2024, its permanent resident population stood at 6,670,400.

九江，古称"柴桑""江州""浔阳"，位于江西西北部，地处长江与京九铁路交会处，是长江中游重要港口城市和沿江开放城市，总面积1.91万平方公里，2024年常住人口449.90万人。

Jiujiang(九江), historically known as Chaisang(柴桑), Jiangzhou(江州),and Xunyang(浔阳), is located in northern Jiangxi at the intersection of the Yangtze River and the Beijing-Kowloon Railway. It is a key port city in the middle reaches of the Yangtze River and an open city along it, covering a total area of 19,100 square kilometers, with a permanent resident population of 4,499,000 in 2024.

景德镇，古称"昌南"，世界闻名的"千年瓷都"，辖1市1县2区及2个功能区，总面积5256平方公里，2024年常住人口161.80万人。

Jingdezhen(景德镇), known as Changnan(昌南) in ancient times, is the world- renowned "Millennium Porcelain Capital". It administers one county- level city, one county, two districts, and two functional zones with a total area of 5,256 square kilometers and a permanent resident population of 1,618,000 in 2024.

萍乡，古称"昭萍"，位于江西西部赣湘交界处，是连接吴楚的交通要道，境内有沪昆高铁和规划中的渝长厦高铁交会，距长沙机场1小时车程，辖2区3县及1个功能区，总面积3823.99平方公里，2024年常住人口179.70万人。

Pingxiang(萍乡), anciently referred to Zhaoping(昭萍),is strategically positioned at the Jiangxi-Hunan border in western Jiangxi, serving as a vital transport corridor connecting the historical states of Wu and Chu. It enjoys exceptional connectivity with the Shanghai-Kunminghigh-speed railway and the planned Chongqing-Xiamen high-speed railway intersecting within its territory, while being merely one hour drive from Changsha Airport. Administratively, it comprises two districts, three counties, and one special economic zone across 3,827 square kilometers with its population census recording 1,797,000 residents in 2024.

新余，古称"新渝"，江西省中西部工业城市，地处南昌、长沙、武汉三角中心，以钢铁和锂电新能源产业著称，是全国唯一国家新能源科技示范城市，辖1区1县，总面积3178平方公里，2024年常住人口119.40万人。

Xinyu(新余), originally named Xinyu(新渝), is an industrial hub in central- western Jiangxi, situated at the pivotal junction among Nanchang,Changsha and Wuhan. Distinguished by its steel production and lithium battery sector, it bears the exclusive title of China's sole National New Energy Technology Demonstration City. The municipality oversees one district and one county across 3,178 square kilometers, housing 1,194,000 residents in 2024.

鹰潭，古称"鹰潭坊"，江西东北部交通枢纽城市，素有"火车拉来的城市"之称，辖1市2区及3个功能区，总面积3560平方公里，2024年常住人口

114.58万人。

Yingtan (鹰潭), initially established as "Yingtanfang"("鹰潭坊"), functions as a critical transport hub in northeastern Jiangxi, famously dubbed as "the railway-spurred city". Its jurisdiction encompasses one county-level city, two districts, plus three special development zones across 3,560 square kilometers, with its census registering 1,145,800 inhabitants in 2024.

赣州,古称"虔州",江西南部中心城市,连接长三角、珠三角经济区,被誉为"客家摇篮",辖18个县(市、区)及多个功能区,总面积3.94万平方公里,2024年常住人口896.06万人。

Ganzhou(赣州), historically called "Qianzhou"(虔州), stands as a central city in southern Jiangxi, bridging the Yangtze River Delta and Pearl River Delta economic zones. Hailed as the "Cradle of Hakka Culture", it manages 18 countylevel divisions and multiple special zones across 39,400 square kilometers with 8,960,600 residents in 2024.

宜春,古称"袁州",江西西北部区域性中心城市,赣湘鄂三省交通枢纽,拥有赣西唯一民用机场,辖10个县(市、区)及3个功能区,总面积1.87万平方公里,2024年常住人口489.88万人。

Yichun(宜春), formerly known as Yuanzhou(袁州), serves as a regional center in northwestern Jiangxi and a critical transportation junction linking Jiangxi, Hunan and Hubei provinces, boasting the only civilian airport in western Jiangxi.It governs 10 county-level divisions (districts/counties/cities) and three special development zones, covering 18,700 square kilometers with 4,898,800 permanent residents in 2024.

上饶,古称"信州",江西东北部"四省通衢"之地,辖12个县(市、区)及3个功能区,总面积2.28万平方公里,2024年常住人口635.09万人。

Shangrao(上饶), formerly called Xinzhou(信州),serves as a crucial interprovincial transit center in northeastern Jiangxi, linking four neighboring provinces.Its administration includes twelve county-level divisions (comprising counties, county-level cities, and districts) along with three special development zones, spanning 22,800 square kilometers with 6,350,900 permanent residents as recorded in 2024.

吉安,古称"庐陵",江西中西部历史文化名城,革命圣地井冈山所在地,素有"江南望郡"美誉,辖13个县(市、区)及2个国家级开发区,总面积2.53万平方公里,2024年常住人口435.07万人。

Ji'an(吉安), historically named Luling (庐陵), is a renowned cultural city in central-western Jiangxi and home to the revolutionary site of Jinggang Mountain. Celebrated as the"Preeminent Prefecture in the South of the Yangtze River", it administers 13 county-level divisions and two national development zones across 25,300 square kilometers, recording 4,350,700 inhabitants in 2024.

抚州,古称"临川",江西东部文化名城,素有"才子之乡"美誉,辖2区9县及2个重点开发区,总面积1.88万平方公里,2024年常住人口353.48万人。

Fuzhou(抚州), historically designated as Linchuan(临川), stands as a culturally famous city in eastern Jiangxi, renowned for centuries as the "Hometown of Talents." Its jurisdiction spans two districts and nine counties complemented by two priority development zones, covering 18,800 square kilometers of territory with a permanent population of 3,534,800 in 2024.

货物贸易进出口总值

Total Value of Goods Imports and Exports

亿元 Hundred Million Yuan

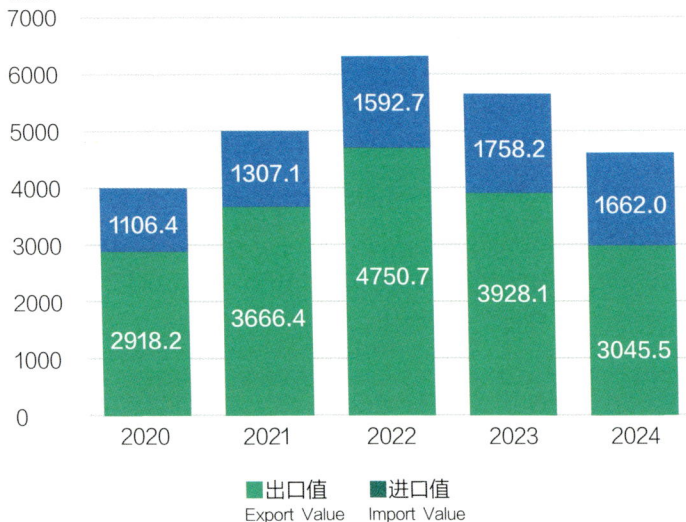

	2020	2021	2022	2023	2024
进口值 Import Value	1106.4	1307.1	1592.7	1758.2	1662.0
出口值 Export Value	2918.2	3666.4	4750.7	3928.1	3045.5

■出口值　　■进口值
Export Value　　Import Value

三次产业增加值占地区生产总值比重

The Proportion of Value Added by the Three Sectors in Regional GDP

%

	2020	2021	2022	2023	2024
第三产业 Tertiary Industry	50.1	50.1	51.5	52.4	52.4
第二产业 Secondary Industry	41.2	42.1	40.7	40.1	40.0
第一产业 Primary Industry	8.7	7.8	7.8	7.5	7.6

■第一产业　　■第二产业　　■第三产业
Primary Industry　　Secondary Industry　　Tertiary Industry

江西地区生产总值及增速

Regional GDP and Growth Rate of Jiangxi

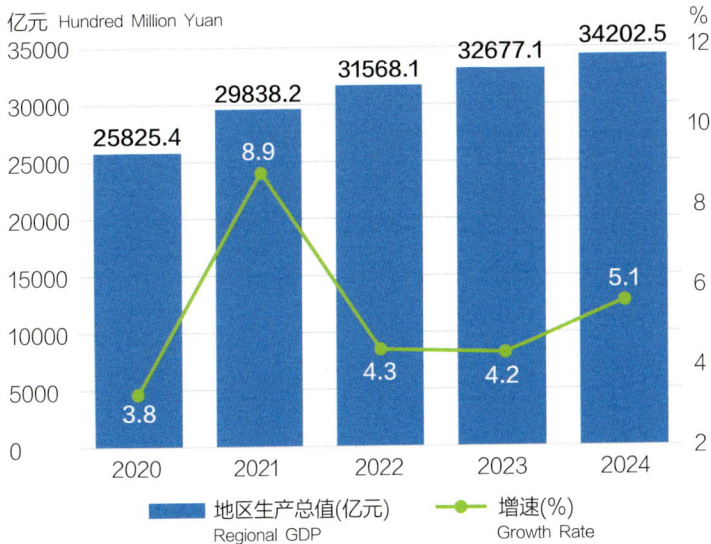

亿元 Hundred Million Yuan

年份	地区生产总值(亿元)	增速(%)
2020	25825.4	3.8
2021	29838.2	8.9
2022	31568.1	4.3
2023	32677.1	4.2
2024	34202.5	5.1

地区生产总值(亿元) Regional GDP ● 增速(%) Growth Rate

目 录
Contents

第一部分 古色
Part I Ancient Jiangxi

赣鄱古韵　风雅千载　弦歌不辍

Ancient Grace of Ganpo (Jiangxi) Echoing Through the Millennia

文化符号 Cultural Symbols 006

古村古建 Ancient Villages and Historic Buildings 032

民俗非遗 Folklore and Intangible Cultural Heritage 044

江西小炒 Jiangxi Stir-Fries 060

第二部分 绿色
Part II Green Jiangxi

美丽江西　山清水秀　风景独好

Beautiful Jiangxi, with Beautiful Mountains and Clear Waters, and Unique Scenery

千山竞绿 Lush Mountains 070

万水皆清 Lucid Waters 084

诗画赣鄱 Pastoral Ganpo(Jiangxi) 092

绿色发展 Green Development 102

第三部分 金色
Part III Golden Jiangxi

金色赣鄱　产经引领　流光溢彩

Prosperous and Abundant Ganpo (Jiangxi)

区位优势 Location Advantages　118

资源禀赋 Resource Endowment　120

特色产业 Featured Industries　122

先进制造 Advanced Manufacturing　136

未来产业 Future Industries　140

第四部分 蓝色
Part IV Blue Jiangxi

心向蔚蓝　包容开放　交流互鉴

Communication and Mutual Learning

国际贸易 International Trade　148

对外投资 Overseas Investment　154

开放平台 Open Platforms　160

营商环境 Business Environment　164

对外交流 Foreign Exchanges　172

第五部分 红色
Part V Red Jiangxi

红土圣地　红色传承　红火生活

Red Sacred Land, Red Inheritance, Flourishing Life

历史坐标 Historical Coordinates　182

红色传承 Red Heritage　188

时代画卷 Scroll of the Era　192

后记 Afterword　208

第一部分

古色

赣鄱古韵
风雅千载
弦歌不辍

Part Ⅰ
Ancient Jiangxi

Ancient Grace of
Ganpo (Jiangxi)
Echoing Through
the Millennia

赣水悠悠，文脉千载。

River Gan flows endlessly, weaving a cultural legacy through the millennia.

江西，赣鄱文化底蕴深厚，陶瓷、书院、戏曲、中医药等享誉古今。

Jiangxi, with its profound Ganpo cultural heritage, boasts a rich legacy renowned across the ages in porcelain, academies, operas, traditional Chinese medicine, etc.

窑火耀古今，世界认识china，从景德镇开始；书院润赣鄱，白鹿洞书院、鹅湖书院、白鹭洲书院等近2000所书院，弦歌不辍；戏腔传南北，江西被誉为戏曲的发源地，是四大声腔之一"弋阳腔"起源之地；客家文化浓，赣州是世界最大的客家人聚居地；杏林根脉长，江西是中医药文化的重要发祥地之一，在中医药界占有重要地位；名流若星辰，涌现了陶渊明、王安石、欧阳修、曾巩、黄庭坚、朱熹、汤显祖、宋应星、朱耷等一大批名家巨匠。

The flame of kiln has illuminated the world history, and "china" was known worldwide from here—Jingdezhen(景德镇); academies nourish the Ganpo (Jiangxi) region, including nearly 2,000 institutions like the Bailudong Academy, Ehu Academy, and Bailuzhou Academy, where scholarship never ceases; opera echoes across the land, as Jiangxi, cradle of traditional Chinese operas, gave birth to Yiyang Opera, one of the four great vocal styles; Hakka culture thrives deeply, with Ganzhou being the largest Hakka settlement worldwide; the apricot grove (symbolizing traditional Chinese medicine) extends its roots, as Jiangxi stands as a pivotal birthplace of traditional Chinese medicine, holding a revered place in history; luminaries shine like stars, including numerous titans of arts and thoughts such as Tao Yuanming, Wang Anshi, Ouyang Xiu, Zeng Gong, Huang Tingjian, Zhu Xi, Tang Xianzu, Song Yingxing, and Zhu Da.

滕王阁、八大山人纪念馆、海昏侯国遗址博物馆等著名景区景点，瓷板画、采茶戏等非物质文化遗产代表性项目，文坛瞩目的江西诗派……数千年来，中国巨擘硕儒吟诵江西，为江西留下了巨大的人文精神与文化财富——王勃的"落霞与孤鹜齐飞，秋水共长天一色"，白居易的"人间四月芳菲尽，山寺桃花始盛开"，文天祥的"人生自古谁无死，留取丹心照汗青"，等等，无不印证着江西文脉绵长，无不彰显着江西"文章节义之邦""人文渊源之地"的光彩。

Lots of legacies bear witness to millennia of intellectual and artistic grandeur, with renowned landmarks like Pavilion of Prince Teng, the Bada Shanren Memorial Hall, Nanchang Relic Museum of Marquis Haihun State of Han Dynasty alongside intangible cultural treasures like porcelain panel paintings and tea-picking opera, and the Jiangxi Poetry School that attracts attention in the literary world. Great minds have long sung of Jiangxi, leaving an indelible imprint on its humanistic legacy like Wang Bo's "The rainbow clouds with lonely bird togather fly; The autumn water blends with endless blue sky"; Bai Juyi's "All flowers in late spring have fallen far and wide,but peach blooms are fullblown on this mountain side"; Wen Tianxiang's "Since olden days there's never been a man but dies,I'd leave a loyalist's name in history only". These verses, etched into time, showcase the brilliance of Jiangxi,known as "the land of literary virtues and righteous martyrs" and "the place of cultural origion".

如今的江西，文化事业蓬勃发展。全省共登记不可移动文物 3.28 万处，其中全国重点文物保护单位 160 处；全省登记认定可移动文物超 64 万件，其中珍贵文物 6.15 万件。一个个闪耀古今的文化符号，铸就了赣鄱文化最深沉、厚重的底色。

Today, Jiangxi's cultural landscape thrives with vitality. The province boasts 32,800 registered immovable cultural relics, including 160 national key cultural relics protection units. Its movable cultural relics inventory exceeds 640,000 pieces, including 61,500 classified as precious artifacts. These shining cultural symbols—bridging ancient and modern times—forge the profound and enduring essence of Ganpo culture, a testament to Jiangxi's legacy as a cradle of Chinese civilization.

赓续千年文脉，赣鄱儿女一路铿锵。

Inheriting millennia-old cultural traditions, the daughters and sons of Jiangxi forge ahead with steadfast determination.

文化符号
Cultural Symbols

镶嵌在大地的记忆

Memories Embedded in the Earth

稻作文化

Rice Cultivation Culture

　　江西,是中国稻作文化的重要发祥地之一。凭借着温暖湿润的气候、纵横交错的河流和肥沃的土壤,江西成为水稻生长的天然沃土,稻作文化在这里孕育发展。

Jiangxi, one of the cradles of China's rice cultivation culture, blessed with a warm, humid climate, a network of rivers, and fertile soils, provides an ideal environment for rice cultivation and gives birth to the rice cultivation culture.

　　万年县素有"鱼米之乡"的美称,其稻作历史可追溯至1万年前。在万年县大源镇的仙人洞和吊桶环遗址中,考古人员发现了距今约1.2万年的稻作遗存,包括稻作植硅石标本等,这些发现为证明中国是世界水稻起源地提供了极为重要的科学证据。万年也因此被考古界认为是世界稻作起源地之一。2021年10月,仙人洞和吊桶环遗址入选中国"百年百大考古发现"。

Wannian County, known as "the land of fish and rice", boasts a rice-cultivating history dating back to 10,000 years ago. Archaeological excavations at the Xianrendong and Diaotonghuan sites in Dayuan Town, Wannian County, have unearthed rice cultivation remains dating back to approximately 12,000 years ago, including phytolith samples of cultivated rice. These discoveries offer pivotal scientific evidence supporting China's claim as the birthplace of rice cultivation, cementing Wannian's status as one of the origions of rice cultivation in the world. In October 2021, the Xianrendong and Diaotonghuan sites were honored as one of China's "Top 100 Archaeological Discoveries of the Century".

　　东汉时期,江西已成为江南地区重要的产粮基地,稻米产量和质量均位居全国前列。元代广丰县尹王祯所著的《王祯农书》,是中国古代"五大农书"之一,系统总结了当时的农业生产经验和技术,涵盖农田水利、作物栽培、农具制造等多个领域。这部著作不仅推动了江西乃至全国农业的发展,也为后世农学研究提供了宝贵的文献资料。

During the Eastern Han dynasty, Jiangxi emerged as a pivotal rice-producing hub in the Jiangnan region, with its rice output and quality ranking among the top nationwide. By the Yuan dynasty, the agricultural expertise of the region was immortalized in Wangzhen Agricultural Book (《王祯农书》), authored by Wang Zhen, magistrate of Guangfeng County. This work, hailed as one of the five great agricultural classics of ancient China, systematically documented farming practices of the era—from irrigation and crop cultivation to tool-making techniques. It not only propelled agricultural advancements in Jiangxi and beyond but also provided invaluable historical documentation for later generations of agronomists.

　　清代,江西的稻作文化达到鼎盛,九江作为中国著名的米市,成为全国粮食贸易的重要枢纽。江西的稻米不仅满足了本地需求,还通过水路运往全国各地,甚至远销海外。

The Qing Dynasty marked the zenith of Jiangxi's rice cultivation legacy. Jiujiang, a bustling rice market, became a national grain trade nexus, channeling Jiangxi's rice surplus to regions across China and even beyond its borders. This era cemented Jiangxi's role as both a granary and a cultural-commercial bridge in the Qing empire's agricultural economy.

青铜文化
Bronze Culture

青铜文明，是华夏文明的见证者。

Bronze civilization stands as a testament to the grandeur of Chinese civilization.

早在商朝时期，江西青铜文化就大放异彩。以樟树吴城遗址和新干大洋洲商墓为代表的考古发现，展现了江南地区青铜文明的辉煌成就。这些遗址所出土的大量精美的青铜器，揭示了古代先民高超的技艺和丰富的文化内涵，为研究中国青铜文明提供了宝贵的实物资料。

As early as the Shang dynasty, Jiangxi's bronze culture burst onto the historical stage. Archaeological discoveries at sites like the Wucheng Site in Zhangshu and the Dayangzhou Shang Dynasty Tomb in Xin'gan have illuminated the brilliance of bronze civilization in the Jiangnan region. The exquisite artifacts unearthed here reveal the mastery of ancient artisans and the profound cultural philosophies embedded in their craft, offering invaluable tangible evidence for the study of China's Bronze Age.

樟树吴城遗址的发掘具有里程碑意义。它是长江以南地区首个年代明确、规模宏大的青铜文化遗址，出土的青铜器以兵器和生产工具为主，包括鼎、尊、斝、矛、戈、剑等，种类繁多，工艺精湛。

The excavation of the Wucheng Site marks a milestone in archaeological history. As southern region of the Yangtze River's first large-scale bronze cultural site with a clearly established chronology, it yielded a trove of artifacts dominated by weapons and equipments including ding (tripod), zun (zun vessels), jia (jia wine vessel), spears, daggers, and swords,etc,with a wide variety of exquisite craftsmanship.

瑞昌市夏畈镇铜岭铜矿遗址，是中国迄今发现的年代最早、保存最完整、内涵最丰富的一处大型矿冶遗址。其开采年代从商代中期延续至战国时期，跨越数百年，展现了古代矿冶技术的辉煌成就。

The Tongling Copper Mine Site in Xiafan, Ruichang, stands as China's earliest, best-preserved, and most archaeologically rich large-scale mining and metallurgical site. Spanning from the mid-Shang dynasty to the Warring States period, it showcases advancements of ancient mining and metallurgical prowess that sustained centuries of extraction.

新干大洋洲商墓的发掘，一举改写了商周时期的江南历史，展现了三千多年前赣江—鄱阳湖流域青铜文明的高度发展。新干大墓出土了大量的青铜器、玉器、陶器等珍贵文物，如伏鸟双尾青铜虎、双面神人青铜面具、屈蹲羽人活环玉佩饰……此墓青铜器数量之多、造型之奇、纹饰之美、铸工之精，为全国所罕见，被誉为"江南青铜王国"。

The excavation of Dayangzhou Shang Dynasty Tomb in Xin'gan, rewrites the history of Jiangnan in the Shang-Zhou era, showcasig the highly developed brone civilization in the Gan River-Poyang Lake Basin. Bronzes, jades, ceramics, and masterpieces like the Crouching Bird-Topped Double-Tailed Tiger, the Double-Faced Divine Human Mask, and the Squatting Feathered Humanoid with Interlocking Rings are unearthed the Xin'gan Tomb.The sheer volume, bizarre forms, exquisite decorations, and flawless casting of these bronzes in the tomb are rare in the country and are known as the "Bronze Kingdom of the Jiangnan region."

陶瓷文化

Ceramic Culture

窑火无声越千年,世界认识中国,从瓷器(china)开始。唐代以前,景德镇叫昌南镇,"china"正是"昌南"的音译。

The silent flame of kilns has endured for millennia, and the world's understanding of China began with porcelain ("china"). Before the Tang Dynasty, Jingdezhen was known as Changnan Town, from which the word "china" originates as a transliteration of its ancient name.

万年仙人洞、吊桶环遗址出土了距今约两万年的陶器,商代鹰潭角山与樟树吴城遗址发掘出原始青瓷。东汉时期,陶瓷技艺逐渐成熟。

Archaeological discoveries at the Xianrendong and Diaotonghuan Sites in Wannian County have unearthed pottery which could be dated back to approximately 20,000 years ago, while primitive celadon ware was excavated from Jiaoshan in Yingtan and Wucheng in Zhangshu in Shang Dynasty. By the Eastern Han dynasty, ceramic crafts-manship had reached mature levels of sophistication.

唐代,洪州窑的青瓷与景德镇的白瓷交相辉映,开启了江西陶瓷的黄金时代。

During the Tang dynasty, the celadon of Hongzhou Kiln and the white porcelain of Jingdezhen marked the dawn of Jiangxi's ceramic golden age.

两宋时期,吉州窑的黑釉瓷深沉古朴,景德镇的影青瓷则"白如玉、明如镜、薄如纸、声如磬",两者各具风韵,成为时代瑰宝。

In the Northen and Southern Song dynasties, the somber elegance of Jizhou Kiln's black-glazed ware contrasted with the "jade-white, mirror-bright, paper-thin, chime-clear" qualities of Jingdezhen's shadowy green porcelain, each embodying distinct aesthetics that became treasures of their era.

元代,景德镇更是迎来了陶瓷艺术的巅峰,青花瓷、青花玲珑瓷、粉彩瓷与颜色釉瓷并称"四大名瓷",奠定了其在全国陶瓷界无可撼动的地位。

The Yuan dynasty witnessed Jingdezhen ascending to the zenith of ceramic artist-ry, with its "Four Famous Porcelains"—blue and white porcelain, blue and white exquisite porcelain, famille-rose porcelain, and colored glaze porcelain—solidifying its unassailable position in China's ceramic industry.

明代,御窑厂落户景德镇,引领着制瓷业走向巅峰,景德镇瓷器远销120多个国家,成为海上丝绸之路的重要贸易品,"世界瓷都"在历史的长河中熠熠生辉。

During the Ming dynasty, the establishment of the imperial porcelain factory in Jing-dezhen propelled porcelain production to unprecedented heights, with Jingdezhen wares being exported to over 120 countries and becoming important commodities along the Maritime Silk Road. This era cemented Jingdezhen as the "World Capital of Porcelain", its brilliance shining through the history.

清代中期之前，景德镇制瓷业依旧处于巅峰，康熙时的郎红、雍正时的粉彩、乾隆时的珐琅彩，各种粉彩瓷争奇斗妍，各种套瓶、交泰瓶、转心瓶等器型精美绝伦。"工匠八方来，器成天下走"是对景德镇制瓷盛况的真实写照。

Prior to the mid-Qing dynasty, the city maintained its ceramic preeminence, with artistic milestones during each emperor's reign: the red-glazed Long ware during Kangxi's reign, the delicate famille-rose porcelain during Yongzheng's reign, and the porcelain with cloisonne enamel during Qianlong's reign. Masterpieces like layered vases, Jiaotai vases, and revolving vases exemplified the pinnacle of craftsmanship. The adage "Artisans converged from all directions, and their creations traveled the world" perfectly encapsulates the scale of Jingdezhen's ceramic prosperity.

一件件耀古烁今的瓷器，凝结着历代工匠的智慧和汗水，成为跨越山海、延绵万里的文明印记。窑火千年，生生不息；陶瓷文化，薪火相传。

Each extraordinary porcelain artifact embodies the wisdom and toil of generations of craftsmen, serving as cultural ambassadors that transcended geographical boundaries. The eternal flame of kiln traditions continues to burn brightly, ensuring the legacy of ceramic culture endures through the ages.

书院文化

Academy Culture

　　自唐代以来，江西建有书院近2000所，占全国总量的四分之一。其中白鹿洞书院、鹅湖书院、白鹭洲书院、象山书院并称江西"四大书院"。而庐山脚下的白鹿洞书院所定院规，成为全国书院治学的规范，影响中国书院文化近千年。位于吉安市内赣江江心的白鹭洲书院，由江万里创办，走出了状元文天祥等大批国之栋梁，至今弦歌不绝。

Since the Tang dynasty, Jiangxi has established nearly 2,000 academies, accounting for a quarter of the national total. Among these, Bailudong Academy, Ehu Academy, Bailuzhou Academy, and Xiangshan Academy are collectively known as the "Four Great Academies in Jiangxi".The regulations formulated by Bailudong Academy at the foot of Mount Lu became a national model for academic governance, shaping Chinese academy culture for nearly a millennium. The Bailuzhou Academy, nestled on the sandbar at the center of River Gan in Ji'an City, was founded by Jiang Wanli and nurtured luminaries like Wen Tianxiang, maintaining an unbroken tradition of scholarship.

　　江西书院的繁荣，推动了江西科举兴盛、人才辈出，"十步之内必有芳草""区区彼江西，其产多材贤"。宋代曾留下"一门十进士""隔河两宰相"的佳话，明代更有"翰林多吉水，朝士半江西"之盛况。据统计，江西历史上共有进士10820人，占全国10.96%；状元31人。

　　The prosperity of Jiangxi's academies promoted the province's golden age of imperial examinations, producing a constellation of talent. People marveled that "within ten paces yielded talented scholars" and Jiangxi earned the praise as "a land brimming with sagehood." The Northern and Southern Song dynasties saw legends like "ten successful candidates come from one family" and "two chancellors on opposite riverbanks." By the Ming dynasty, the adage "Hanlin academicians thrived in Jishui, while half the court officials hailed from Jiangxi" epitomized Jiangxi's intellectual dominance. Historical records show Jiangxi produced 10,820 imperial scholars (jinshi,进士), comprising 10.96% of the national total, and 31 top scholars (zhuangyuan, 状元).

　　赣鄱大地俊采星驰：以节义论，有胡铨、洪皓、江万里、文天祥、谢枋得等；以文学论，有欧阳修、曾巩、王安石、黄庭坚、杨万里、晏几道、姜夔、洪迈等；以哲学论，有朱熹、陆九渊、李觏、吴澄、吴与弼、何心隐等。这些硕彦名儒，定义了江西人的精神高度、人文厚度，是中国文化、中国气象的重要载体。

　　This fertile soil nurtured luminaries across disciplines: paragons of moral integrity like Hu Quan, Hong Hao, Jiang Wanli, Wen Tianxiang, and Xie Fangde; literary giants like Ouyang Xiu, Zeng Gong, Wang Anshi, Huang Tingjian, Yang Wanli, Yan Jidao, Jiang Kui, and Hong Mai; and philosophical masters like Zhu Xi, Lu Jiuyuan, Li Gou, Wu Cheng, Wu Yubi, and He Xinyin. These towering figures defined Jiangxi's intellectual ethos and cultural depth, embodying the essence of Chinese civilization and its enduring spirit.

中医药文化

Traditional Chinese Medicine Culture

江西,中医药重要发祥地与昌盛之域,其医药史源远流长,自先秦萌芽,经秦汉兴起、隋唐发展、宋元繁盛,至明清渐趋稳固,书写了中国医药史上的璀璨篇章。

Jiangxi, a cradle and flourishing domain of Traditional Chinese Medicine (TCM), boasts a profound medical heritage that traces back to pre-Qin times. Through successive dynastic developments—rising in Qin and Han dynasties, evolving in Sui and Tang dynasties, prospering in Song and Yuan dynasties, and stabilizing in Ming and Qing dynasties—it has etched a glorious chapter in China's medical history.

杏林文化独具神韵。三国时,名医董奉于庐山潜心修道行医,始终秉持着"患者病愈后,有资者付酬,无资者植杏一株"的治病理念。久之,杏树成林,"杏林"便成为医界的别称。

The Apricot Grove Culture embodies a unique spiritual charm. During the Three Kingdoms period, renowned physician Dong Feng cultivated Daoist practices and medicine on Mount Lu, adhering to the principle: "For cured patients, let the affluent pay, while the indigent plant an apricot tree." Over time, these trees formed a veritable forest, with "Apricot Grove" becoming a metonym for the medical profession.

盱江医学声名远播。它发轫于抚州南城。据统计,盱江流域所涉县市存有古代医家1200余人、医籍700余种。于全国历代62家针灸学派里,盱江医家独占8家。

Xujiang(盱江) Medicine commands widespread acclaim. Originating in Nancheng, Fuzhou, this school boasts over 1,200 ancient medical practitioners and 700 medical texts recorded across Xujiang River basin counties. Among China's 62 historical acupuncture schools, eight originated from Xujiang medical circles.

樟树药都闻名遐迩。明时,樟树便在药王庙设药材交易之所。此地遂成南北、

川广药材汇聚要地，而樟树则享有"中国药都"之美誉。明末清初，樟树中药铺数量猛增，达200余家，且形成颇具影响力的"樟树药帮"，民间则流传"药不到樟树不齐，药不过樟树不灵"。

"Medicine Capital" Zhangshu (樟树) has become famous all over the world. During the Ming dynasty, Zhangshu established medicinal herb markets at the Temple of the Medicine King (药王庙), becoming a convergence point for medicinal materials from northern–southern China and Sichuan-Guangxi regions—earning its title as "China's Medicine Capital." From the late Ming to early Qing period, over 200 pharmacies thrived here, forming the influential "Zhangshu Medical Guild." A folk saying attests: "Medicines remain incomplete until they reach Zhangshu; their efficacy falters without Zhangshu's refinement."

江西名医辈出，熠熠生辉。内科圣手董奉，善扶危救急，与张仲景、华佗并称"建安三神医"；万氏儿科之万全，与李时珍齐名，首倡小儿"三有余、四不足"论；蔺道人所著《仙授理伤续断秘方》，为我国首部骨伤科专著；危亦林的《世医得效方》，为我国首部正骨学专著，对骨伤科证治载述尤详。

Jiangxi has been renowned for producing numerous distinguished physicians who shine brilliantly throughout history. Among them, Dong Feng, a master of internal medicine, excelled in rescuing patients from critical conditions and was honored as one of the "Three Eminent Physicians of the Jian'an Era," alongside Zhang Zhongjing and Hua Tuo. Wan Quan, a leading figure in pediatrics and a peer of Li Jinzhen, pioneered the theory of "Three Excesses and Four Deficiencies" in pediatrics. Lin Daoren authored *Immortal-Taught Secret Formulas for Treating Wounds and Setting Fractures* (*Xianshou Lishang Xuduan Mifang*), the first medical text specialized on orthopedics and traumatology in China. Additionally, Wei Yilin compiled *Effective Formulas from Generations of Physicians* (*Shiyi Dexiao Fang*), the earliest treatise on bone-setting in China, which provides an exceptionally detailed account of the diagnosis and treatment of orthopedic and traumatological conditions.

戏曲文化

Opera Culture

江西戏曲文化源远流长，丰厚的历史文化孕育了独具特色的戏曲剧种。

Jiangxi boasts a profound and long-standing opera tradition, nurtured by its rich historical and cultural heritage, giving rise to distinctive regional opera genres.

赣剧，是江西戏曲的代表性剧种，国家级非物质文化遗产代表性项目。它由赣东北的饶河戏和信河戏融合而成，以弋阳腔为声腔基础。赣剧唱腔高亢激昂，兼具粗犷与细腻之美。其剧目多取材于历史故事和民间传说，如《三国传》《岳飞传》等，极具文化底蕴和艺术魅力。

Gan Opera is the representative opera of Jiangxi and a representative project of National Intangible Cultural Heritage. It derived from the fusion of Raohe Opera and Xinhe Opera in northeastern Jiangxi, with Yiyang Tune as its vocal foundation. Gan Opera features bold, resonant singing that combines both vigor and delicacy. Its repertoire often draws from such historical tales and folk legends as Three Kingdoms Legend, Legend of Yue Fei, etc., showcasing deep cultural significance and artistic charm.

作为赣剧声腔基础的弋阳腔，是中国高腔戏曲的鼻祖，对全国40多个剧种的形成产生了深远影响。其演唱方式独特，采用"徒歌、帮腔"形式，以锣鼓伴奏，戏剧性和表现力极强。

Yiyang Tune, the cornerstone of Gan Opera's vocal style, is considered the origin of high-pitched Chinese opera and has profoundly influenced the formation of over 40 opera genres across China. Its performance style is distinctive, featuring a cappella singing with choral accompaniment (bangqiang) and accompany by gongs and drums, delivering strong dramatic and expressive power.

此外，江西还有东河戏、宜黄戏、盱河戏、西河戏、宁河戏等剧种。

Beyond Gan Opera, Jiangxi is home to other regional operas, including Donghe Opera, Yihuang Opera, Xuhe Opera, Xihe Opera, and Ninghe Opera.

江西戏曲的繁荣离不开两位杰出的戏曲家——汤显祖和蒋士铨。

汤显祖被誉为"东方莎士比亚"，其代表作"临川四梦"（《紫钗记》《牡丹亭》《邯郸记》《南柯记》）以爱情为主题，融入了"梦"的意象，艺术成就极高，不仅在国内广受欢迎，还远播海外，成为世界戏剧艺术的瑰宝。

蒋士铨则是清代戏曲的集大成者，被誉为"中国戏曲史上的殿军"，其"藏园九种曲"如《临川梦》《冬青树》等，展现了深厚的文学功底和戏曲创作才华。

The flourishing of Jiangxi's opera culture owes much to two eminent playwrights—Tang Xianzu and Jiang Shiquan.

Tang Xianzu, hailed as the "Shakespeare of the East", is best known for his masterpiece "The Four Dreams of Linchuan" (The Purple Hairpins, The Peony Pavilion, The Handan Dream, and The Nanke Dream). These works explore themes of love through the motif of dreams, achieving unparalleled artistic heights. They have not only gained immense popularity in China but also spread worldwide, becoming treasures of global theatrical art.

Jiang Shiquan marked the culmination of Qing Dynasty opera and has been regarded as the "last among the great figures in Chinese opera history". His "Nine Plays from the Hidden Garden", including Dream in Linchuan and The Wintergreen Tree, demonstrate his profound literary skill and exceptional talent in opera composition.

客家文化

Hakka Culture

江西是客家文化的重要发祥地与核心区域之一。尤其是赣南地区，在语言、建筑、民俗和精神内涵等方面，展现了客家人深厚的历史底蕴与独特的文化魅力。

Jiangxi is one of the most important birthplaces and core regions of Hakka culture, particularly in southern Jiangxi (赣南), where the Hakka people's profound historical heritage and unique cultural charm are reflected in their language, architecture, folk traditions, and spiritual values.

客家话，被誉为"古汉语的活化石"，是客家文化的重要载体。它保留了大量的古汉语词汇和发音特点，仿佛一座跨越千年的语言桥梁，连接着古代与现代。

Hakka dialect, hailed as "a living fossil of ancient Chinese," serves as a vital vessel of Hakka culture. Preserving a wealth of archaic Chinese vocabulary and phonetic features. It functions as a linguistic bridge spanning millennia, connecting antiquity with modernity.

客家建筑，以围屋最为典型。客家围屋多为方形或圆形，外墙高大厚实，内部布局紧凑。赣南客家围屋主要分布在江西省赣州市，包括龙南关西围屋群、燕翼围、渔仔潭围和乌石围，全南雅溪围屋群，定南虎形围和明远第围，安远东生围屋群等。赣南客家围屋集祠、家、堡于一体，具有鲜明的防卫特征和宗族群居的亲和性。它们是客家人智慧的丰碑，是赣南文化的瑰宝。它们见证了客家人的奋斗历程，承载着客家人的精神追求。

Hakka architecture is epitomized by the enclosed house. Predominantly square or circular in shape, these structures feature stout exterior walls and compact interior layouts. Gannan's Hakka enclosed houses cluster primarily in Ganzhou City, Jiangxi Province, including notable complexes such as the Longnan Guanxi Enclosed House Cluster, Yanyi Enclosure, Yuzaitan Enclosure, and Wushi Enclosure in Longnan County; the Yaxi Enclosed House Cluster in Quannan County; the Tiger-shaped Enclosure and Mingyuandi Enclosure in Dingnan County; and the Dongsheng Enclosed House Cluster in Anyuan County. Integrating ancestral temples, residential spaces, and fortifications, these structures exhibit distinct defensive capabilities and communal clan living arrangements. They stand as monuments to Hakka wisdom and treasures of Gannan culture, bearing witness to generations of Hakka perseverance while embodying their spiritual aspirations.

此外，赣南客家人还保留了许多传统手工艺，如客家剪纸、竹编、刺绣等。这些技艺不仅是文化的传承，更是客家人智慧的结晶，为这片土地增添了独特的艺术气息。

In addition, the Gannan Hakka community has preserved numerous traditional handicrafts, such as Hakka paper-cutting, bamboo plaiting, and embroidery. These crafts serve not only as cultural heritage but also as the crystallization of Hakka ingenuity, imbuing this land with a distinctive artistic aura.

宗教文化

Religious Culture

江西是佛、道两教的开源播流之地。

Jiangxi stands as the cradle for the dissemination of Buddhism and Daoism in China.

禅宗"一花开五叶，三叶在江西"。"马祖建道场，百丈立清规"，佛教中国化的两件大事都发生在江西宜春。"马祖建道场"解决了佛教中国化的硬件问题，"百丈立清规"解决了佛教中国化的软件问题。江西云居山真如禅寺自唐代以来高僧辈出，中国佛教协会成立后的六任会长中，一诚大师、传印大师三任会长来自该寺。

In the realm of Zen Buddhism, the adage "One flower blossoms into five petals, three of which thrive in Jiangxi" underscores Jiangxi's profound influence. Two pivotal milestones in the sinicization of Buddhism unfolded in Yichun, Jiangxi: "Mazu Established Bodhimanda, and Baizhang Formulated Monastic Rules". The former addressed the structural adaptation of Buddhism to China, while the latter institutionalized its behavioral codes. Mount Yunju's Zhenru Zen Monastery has nurtured generations of eminent monks since the Tang dynasty, including two presidents of the Buddhist Association of China—Yicheng, and Chuanyin.

名山古刹是禅宗文化的重要载体。庐山东林寺，吸引了无数高僧大德在此修行弘法；云居山真如禅寺是曹洞宗祖庭之一，至今仍是禅修的重要场所；百丈山百丈寺则是百丈怀海禅师弘扬禅法之地。此外，南昌西山、樟树阁皂山、上饶三清山、南城麻姑山等地也是著名的宗教文化胜地。南昌佑民寺、宜黄曹山寺、靖安宝峰寺等寺庙也在中国佛教发展史上占有重要地位。

Sacred mountains and ancient temples serve as vital carriers of Zen culture. Mount Lu's Donglin Temple has attracted countless masters to practice dharma; Zhenru Zen Temple on Mount Yunju, an ancestral temple of the Caodong School, remains a key center for Zen meditation; Baizhang Temple on Mount Baizhang is where Master Baizhang Huaihai expounded Zen teachings. Other notable religious sites include Nanchang's Xishan Mountain, Zhangshu's Gezao Mountain, Shangrao's Mount Sanqing, and Nancheng's Magu Mountain. Temples like Youmin Temple in Nanchang, Caoshan Temple in Yihuang, and Baofeng Temple in Jing'an hold significant positions in the history of Chinese Buddhism.

道教文化在这里发源。东汉中叶，张道陵在江西龙虎山创立了道教正一派，龙虎山也因此被誉为"千年道教祖庭"，"南张（张天师）北孔（孔夫子）"成为中国文化史上独有的千年世家。《水浒传》开篇故事"张天师祈禳瘟疫，洪太尉误走妖魔"，就发生在龙虎山。

Jiangxi is also the birthplace of Daoist culture. In the Eastern Han dynasty, Zhang Daoling founded the Daoist Zhengyi School at Mount Longhu in Jiangxi, earning the mountain the title of "Millennial Cradle of Daoism." The "Celestial Master Zhang Tianshi" of the south and the Confucius' lineage in the north constitute the unique millennia-old aristocratic lineages in Chinese cultural history. The opening chapter of The Water Margin recounts the tale "Celestial Master Zhang Tianshi Quells Pestilence,and Imperial Commissioner Hong Releases Demons," which took place precisely at Mount Longhu.

江西诗派

Jiangxi Poetry School

江西诗派是中国文学史上第一个有正式名称的诗文流派，兴起于北宋后期，以黄庭坚为核心，影响深远，贯穿宋元明清，直至近代。

The Jiangxi Poetry School stands as the first formally named literary school in the history of Chinese literature, emerging in the late Northern Song dynasty and centered around Huang Tingjian. Its influence permeated the Song, Yuan, Ming, and Qing dynasties, even into modern times.

黄庭坚，九江修水人，宋代著名的诗人、词人和书法家，与陈师道、陈与义并称江西诗派"三宗"。他以其独特的诗风和理论主张，吸引了众多追随者，于是一个以江西籍诗人为主的诗歌流派逐渐形成。

Huang Tingjian, a native of Xiushui, Jiujiang, was a renowned poet, lyricist, and calligrapher of the Song dynasty. Together with Chen Shidao and Chen Yuyi, they were known as "Three Masters" of the Jiangxi Poetry School. His distinctive poetic style and theoretical propositions attracted numerous followers, gradually forming a poetry school mainly composed of poets from Jiangxi.

江西诗派不仅在北宋诗坛占据重要地位，其影响还遍及整个南宋诗坛，并延续至元、明、清各代。近代的"同光体"诗人，如陈三立、陈衍、沈曾植等，也深受其影响。

The school not only held a pivotal position in Northern Song poetry, but its influence also spread its reach across the Southern Song dynasty, leaving an indelible mark on the poetry of the Yuan, Ming, and Qing periods. Even modern "Tongguang Style" poets,

including Chen Sanli, Chen Yan, and Shen Zengzhi, drew profound inspiration from its legacy.

江西诗派的理论和实践，为中国古典诗歌的发展注入了新的活力，成为中国诗歌史上不可忽视的重要篇章。其注重学问、讲究技巧的创作理念，以及对诗歌艺术的深刻探索，对后世文人产生了深远的影响，奠定了其在中国文学史上的重要地位。

The Jiangxi Poetry School injected fresh vitality into the evolution of Chinese classical poetry, becoming an indispensable chapter in the nation's poetic history. Its emphasis on scholarly erudition, technical mastery, and profound artistic exploration has exerted a lasting impact on later generations of poets, solidifying its important place in Chinese literary history.

江西画派

Jiangxi Painting School

江西画派，中国画流派之一，是清初一个享誉全国的书画团体，对后世画坛产生了重大影响。

The Jiangxi Painting School, a school of Chinese painting, emerged as a renowned calligraphic and painting group during the early Qing dynasty, leaving a significant impact on the art world of later generations.

画家们常以江西的山水风物为题材，将赣地的灵秀与厚重融入笔端。他们的画作中，既有庐山云雾的缥缈，也有鄱阳湖水的浩渺，更有赣南丘陵的苍翠。这些画作不仅展现了江西的自然之美，也承载了画家们对故土的深情。

Artists of this school frequently drew inspiration from Jiangxi's natural scenery and cultural heritage, infusing their works with the ethereal beauty and profound character of the region. Their paintings captured the mist-shrouded grandeur of Mount Lu, the boundless expanse of Poyang Lake, and the emerald hills of southern Jiangxi. These paintings not only celebrated the province's natural wonders but also embodied the artists' deep affection for their homeland.

罗牧是江西画派的重要代表人物之一，他以山水画见长，风格清逸淡远，笔墨自然流畅。晚年，罗牧与好友八大山人在南昌东湖畔创立"东湖书画会"，成员包括为书风格酷似黄庭坚的徐煌、工董其昌书法

的熊秉哲，还有彭廷谟、李仍、蔡秉质、涂岫、闵应铨、齐鉴、吴雯炯、朱容重等人。他们将江西画派的艺术精神发扬光大，使得这一流派在中国画坛上占据了举足轻重的地位。

Among the school's luminaries, Luo Mu distinguished himself as a master of land-scape painting, celebrated for his elegant, distant styles and fluid, natural brushwork. In his later years, Luo Mu co-founded the "East Lake Painting and Calligraphy Association" alongside his friend Bada Shanren on the shores of Nanchang's East Lake. The association attracted prominent figures such as Xu Huang (renowned for his calligraphy reminiscent of Huang Tingjian), Xiong Bingzhe (a master of Dong Qichang's calligraphic style), as well as Peng Tingmo, Li Reng, Cai Bingzhi, Tu Xiu, Min Yingquan, Qi Jian, Wu Wenjiong, Zhu Rongzhong, and others. Together, they carried forward the artistic spirit of the Jiangxi Painting School, solidifying its pivotal role in the Chinese painting world.

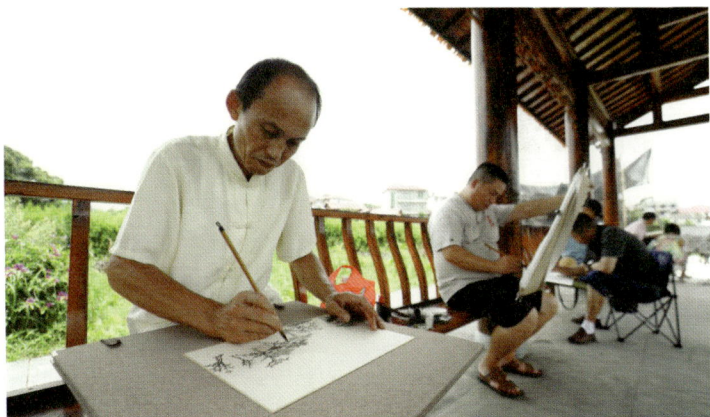

古村古建
Ancient Villages and Historic Buildings

活着的文物与历史

Living cultural relics and history

江西古村落、古建筑星罗棋布。它们像一颗颗璀璨的明珠，撒播在广袤无垠的赣鄱大地上，成为凝固在时光里的乡愁。

Ancient villages and historic buildings dot the landscape of Jiangxi Province like a constellation of shimmering pearls scattered across the vast expanse of the Ganpo region, embodying a nostalgia frozen in time.

千里赣江第一县赣县，成群的白鹭在古朴的白鹭古村翩翩起舞；流坑的古祠堂，庄严肃穆中透着家族传承的厚重；安义古村的明清建筑群，飞檐翘角间流淌着匠人的巧思……这些村落，或依山傍水而建，或与自然和谐共生，展现着江西先民"天人合一"的智慧。

Flocks of egrets dance gracefully above the time-honored village Bailu (Egret) in Gan County, which has been hailed as the "First County along the Thousand-li Gan River". At Village Liukeng, ancient ancestral halls exude an air of solemnity, bearing witness to the weighty legacy of familial lineage. In Ancient Village Anyi, building complex of the Ming and Qing dynasties showcases the ingenuity of craftsmen through upturned eaves

and intricate carvings... These villages, nestled beside mountains or rivers or harmoniously integrated with nature, manifest the profound wisdom of Jiangxi's ancestors in their pursuit of "harmony of man with nature."

江西古建筑的精妙之处,在于其独特的营造技艺,影响较大的是"样式雷"。"样式雷"是中国古代建筑科技史上成就卓著的杰出代表,创造了5项"世界文化遗产"和1项"世界记忆遗产",是全世界唯一一获此殊荣的建筑世家。故宫、天坛、颐和园、承德避暑山庄和明清皇陵的清东陵、清西陵等建筑物出自"样式雷"。

The exquisite craftsmanship of Jiangxi's ancient architecture is epitomized by the "royal architects Lei's clan", a preeminent lineage in the history of ancient Chinese architectural technology. Lei's clan created five "World Cultural Heritage Sites" and one "Memory of the World," the sole architectural family in the world achieving such honors. Their masterpieces include the Forbidden City, the Temple of Heaven, the Summer Palace, Chengde Mountain Resort, and the Eastern and Western Tombs of the Qing dynasty of the Ming and Qing imperial mausoleums.

此外,榫卯结构的精妙运用,让建筑历经数百年风雨依然巍然屹立;藻井、斗拱等构件的精美雕刻,将实用与审美完美统一;马头墙的起伏错落,既防火防风,又形成独特的美学韵律……

Moreover, the ingenious application of mortise and tenon joint enables these structures to withstand centuries of weathering while standing resolute. Exquisite carvings on components such as domed coffered ceilings and bracket systems seamlessly unite functionality with aesthetic appeal. The undulating patterns of horse-head walls serve dual purposes—mitigating fire and wind hazards while forming a distinctive aesthetic rhythm...

如今,这些古村古建,在保护与开发并重的理念下,不再是静止的历史标本,而是活态的文化载体。游客在这里感受乡愁,学者在这里探寻历史,艺术家在这里寻找灵感……它们正以其独特的魅力,讲述着江西故事,传承着中华文明。

Nowadays, guided by the principle of balancing preservation and development, these ancient villages and architectures are no longer static historical specimens but living cultural carriers. Tourists experience nostalgia here, scholars probe into history, and artists seek inspiration... With their unique allure, the ancient villages and architectures narrate the tales of Jiangxi and perpetuate the heritage of Chinese civilization.

白鹭古村

Ancient Village Bailu

　　白鹭古村位于赣州市赣县区的最北端,距赣州市区约63公里,毗邻兴国和万安,全村总面积约1平方公里。白鹭建村距今约890年,共有人口近3000人,其中98%姓钟。白鹭村是千年客家第一村,村内原有近6万平方米的古建筑,其中保存较完好的古祠堂、古民居有69栋,是江西省保存较完整、较集中、气势恢宏的一处客家古代商业集镇和客家古民居群,素有"明清古建筑活博物馆"之称,其中兴复堂、世昌堂、恢烈公祠、王太夫人祠等被列为省级文物保护单位。白鹭古村先后获评"中国历史文化名村""中国十大古村"等荣誉。

Ancient Village Bailu, located at the northernmost end of Ganxian District, Ganzhou City, Jiangxi Province, sits approximately 63 kilometers away from Ganzhou city. Bordered by Xingguo County and Wan'an County, the village spans a total area of about 1 square kilometer. Founded over 890 years ago, Village Bailu is home to a population of nearly 3,000 residents, 98% of which bear the surname Zhong. Renowned as the "first representative village" in the one thousand years of Hakka history, Bailu once boasted nearly 60,000 square meters of ancient buildings. Among these, 69 well-preserved ancestral temples and vernacular residences remain standing, constituting one of the most intact, concentrated, and architecturally magnificent Hakka commercial settlements and residential clusters in the province. Often hailed as a "living museum of Ming and Qing dynasties' architectural heritage", the village's cultural treasures include four official provincial-level monuments and sites: Xingfu Hall, Shichang Hall, Huilie Ancestral Shrine, and Madam Wang's Ancestral Shrine. Ancient Village Bailu has been awarded honors such as "Famous Historical and Cultural Village in China " and "Top Ten Ancient Villages in China".

安义古村

Ancient Village Anyi

安义古村位于南昌市郊西山梅岭脚下，距南昌市区60公里，是赣派建筑村落之一。安义古村古建筑群主要分布于罗田、水南、京台三大自然村。

Ancient Village Anyi, located at the foot of Meiling Mountain in Mount Xi, western suburb of Nanchang City, Jiangxi Province, sits 60 kilometers away from Nanchang city proper. As one of the Gan-style architectural villages in the region, its historic architectural clusters are primarily distributed across three natural villages: Luotian, Shuinan, and Jingtai.

以士大夫第、曦庐为代表的典型赣派风格明清建筑恢宏壮观：三重进五重进主体、天井、纵横的厅堂、石刻门楣、雕镂门窗，无不让人赞叹古人当时高超的建筑水平和精湛的雕刻技艺。民俗馆中年代久远的生产生活用具、古戏台随声摆动的斗拱、墨庄弥漫的书香、沿街林立的古商铺，处处浸透着古村独特的赣文化与赣商

文化的韵味。

The village's typical Gan-style architecture of the Ming and Qing dynasties, exemplified by the Scholar Officials' Residences and Xilu Mansion, showcase the grandeur of Gan-style architecture: triple and quintuple courtyard layouts, patios, interconnected halls, stone-carved lintels, and intricately carved doors and windows. These structures attest to the ancient people's exceptional craftsmanship and architectural sophistication during its heyday. The Folklore Museum displays ancient farming tools and household artifacts, the swaying bracket sets synchronized with performers' movements on the ancient stage, the fragrance books that excludes from ink studies, and ancient shopfronts lining the streets.These exhibits permeate the village with a unique blend of Jiangxi's cultural heritage and Gan merchant culture.

安义古村现有明清时期的古民居建筑86幢,规模宏大、保存完整、雕饰精美、文化内涵厚重。

Ancient Village Anyi currently preserves 86 vernacular residences of Ming and Qing dynasties, distinguished by their massive scale, intact preservation, exquisite carvings, and cultural profoundity.

流坑古村

Ancient Village Liukeng

流坑古村位于抚州市乐安县,始建于五代南唐,以董姓聚居为主。因董氏科第而兴旺,时有"一门五进士,两朝四尚书,文武两状元,秀才若繁星"的美誉。流坑古村先后被评为首批中国传统村落、中国首批历史文化名村、全国生态文化村和中国美丽休闲乡村,并入选"中国最具潜力的十大古镇"。

Ancient Village Liukeng, located in Le'an County, Fuzhou City, Jiangxi Province, traces its origin to the Southern Tang dynasty of the Five Dynasties and Ten Kingdoms period. It is predominantly inhabited by the Dong clan, whose scholarly and official achievements propelled the village to prominence, earning it the laudatory title: "Five Im-

perial Scholars in one Family, Four Ministers Across Two Dynasties, Two Grand Champions (Civil and Military), and Scholars As Numerous as the Stars." Liukeng has been honored as one of the first Traditional Chinese Villages, National Famous Historic and Cultural Villages, National Ecological Culture Villages, and Chinese Beautiful Leisure Villages. It was also selected among "China's Ten Most Promising Ancient Towns."

古村四周青山环抱，三面江水绕流，错落有致的古建筑分布在一条条巷道两旁，青砖黛瓦，古朴典雅。近年来，依托农耕、民俗等文化，流坑古村将传统村落保护与文旅产业发展有机融合，流坑"千古第一村"这张名片越擦越亮。

Surrounded by verdant mountains, the ancient village is cradled by meandering rivers on three sides. The villages meticulously arranged ancient buildings scatter on both sides of the alleys, with blue bricks and black tiles exuding an antiquated elegance. In recent years, Liukeng has pioneered a model of integrating heritage conservation with cultural tourism, elevating its reputation as "China's Foremost Ancient Village of Timeless Legacy."

钓源古村

Ancient Village Diaoyuan

　　钓源古村位于吉安市吉州区，距吉安城区 17 公里。古村始建于唐朝末年，是北宋著名政治家、文学家欧阳修的后裔及同宗聚居地。古村现存风姿各异的赣派明清建筑 150 余幢，它们依山就势，布局如八卦。村内有一条高约 9 米、蜿蜒千米、呈东西走向的"S"形山脉，上植 2 万余株古樟树，形似道家太极图。村中东高西低七个池塘一字相连，取"七星伴月"之意。

　　Ancient Village Diaoyuan, located in Jizhou District, Ji'an City, Jiangxi Province, sits 17 kilometers away from Ji'an's urban area. Founded in the late Tang dynasty, it served as the ancestral settlement and kinship stronghold of Ouyang Xiu, a celebrated Northern Song politician, and writer. The village preserves over 150 buidings of the Gan-style from Ming and Qing dynasties, whose layouts mirror the Eight Trigrams formation, with structures adapting to the hillside topography. There is an S-shaped mountain range in the village that is about nine meters high, winding for kilometers, and runs east-west. More than 20,000 ancient camphor trees are planted on the mountain, resembling the Taoist Tai Ji diagram. Seven interconnected ponds, descending from east to west, symbolize the "Seven Stars Accompanying the Moon".

　　历史上，生活在钓源的欧阳氏人才辈出，共有 9 人进士及第，有举人 32 位。到清代中叶，钓源商贾、店铺遍及两湖两广，富甲一方；村内建有大批祠堂、牌坊、书院、别墅、民居；茶楼酒肆林立，店铺连街，俨然一个乡村都会。

　　Historically, the Ouyang clan of Diaoyuan produced numerous talented individuals, including nine palace graduates and 32 provincial graduates. By the mid-Qing dynasty, Diaoyuan's merchants and shops were spread throughout Hubei, Hunan, Guangdong,

and Guangxi. There are a large number of ancestral halls, memorial arches, academies, villas, and folk residences. Tea houses, taverns, and shops line its streets, transforming the village into a rural metropolis.

如今的钓源古村景区，运用村庄的巷弄空间，收集曾经、现在的人们在钓源村的生活轨迹，深度解析钓源村的历史文化；以"村"为单位，整体策划一个以欧阳氏村落生活记忆为主的文化展，同时落地成为国内首个沉浸式的穿越巷弄的乡村博物馆。

Today, the Diaoyuan Ancient Village Scenic Area utilizes its alleyways to collect the life trajectories of pepole in Diaoyuan Village, both past and present, and deeply analyze the historical and cultural significance of the village; The village has planned a cultural exhibition centered around the memorise of Ouyang clan's village life, using the "village" as a unit, and establish it as the first immersive rual museum in China that spans through allays.

渼陂古村

Ancient Village Meibei

渼陂古村位于吉安市青原区文陂镇富水河畔，是一座集农商文化、书院文化、祠堂文化、宗教文化、红色文化和明清雕刻艺术于一体的古村，被誉为将军村、庐陵文化第一村，是中国历史文化名村。

Ancient Village Meibei, located in Wenbei Town, Qingyuan District, Ji'an City, Jiangxi Province, sits along the Fushui River and stands as an ancient village that integrates agrarian- merchant traditions, academy culture, ancestral hall heritage, religious culture, red culture, and Ming-Qing carving arts. Renowned as the "Village of Generals" and "Premier Settlement of Luling Culture", it is a National Famous Historical and Cultural Village of China.

渼陂村由梁氏祖先开基于南宋初年，距今近900年历史。芗峰东立，象岭西护，紫瑶南耸，富水北流。村中明清建筑367栋，有民居、祠堂、书院、庙宇、码头等。古建筑的门楣、藻井、窗棂、门柱、影壁、山墙，或为书画，或为雕刻，内容不同、风格各异，反映出不同的时代风貌和不同主人的情趣爱好。其中总祠永慕堂，占地一千多平方米，翘角飞檐，镂花斗拱，红石檐柱，雕刻精美。

Founded by the Liang clan ancestors in the early Southern Song dynasty, Meibei has a history of nearly 900 years. Xiangfeng Peak stands to the east, Xiangling Ridge stands to the west, Ziyao Mountain rises to the south, and the Fushui River flows north-

ward. The village preserves 367 buildings from Ming and Qing dynasties, including folk residences, ancestral halls, academies, temples, and wharves. Architectural details,such as lintels, domed coffered ceilings, window grilles,door posts, screen walls, and gables, are either painted or carved ,with different contents and styles,reflecting different historical styles and owners' aesthetic sensibilities. Among these, the Yongmu Ancestral Hall spans more than 1,000 square meters and showcases upturned eaves, carved bracketing, red-stone pillars, and equisite carvings.

渼陂村耕读传家,人文荟萃,宋元培养出太常博士梁昭伯、江州教授梁君庸等人才,被文天祥称为"文献名宗""衣冠望族"。

Meibei's legacy of "cultivation through farming and scholarship" has nurtured talents across eras, including Liang Zhaobo, a Taichang Academy doctorate during the Song and Yuan dynasties, and Liang Junyong, a Jiangzhou- region scholar.Meibei was praised by Wen Tianxiang as a place famous of its academic and moral traditions.

民俗非遗
Folklore and Intangible Cultural Heritage

散落在民间的风雅
The Elegance Scattered among the People

嘹亮的山歌、古老的跳傩、独具特色的剪纸……江西民俗非遗是赣鄱文化的多彩呈现。

Resounding mountain airs, ancient Nuo dance rituals, and unique handmade paper-cutting… Jiangxi's folklore and intangible cultural heritage is a vibrant tapestry of Ganpo culture.

从传统节庆到民间艺术,从手工技艺到戏曲表演,江西民俗非遗以其独特的地域特色和深厚的文化内涵,成为连接过去与未来的文化纽带。

From traditional festivals to folk arts, from craftsmanship techniques to opera performances, Jiangxi's folklore and intangible cultural heritage, with its unique regional characteristics and profound cultural connotations, serves as a cultural bridge between past and future.

江西共有88项国家级非物质文化遗产代表性项目、560项省级非遗代表性项目,有国家级非遗传承人69人、各级非遗传承人7000余人,涵盖民间文学、传统音乐、传统舞蹈、传统戏剧、曲艺、传统体育、游艺与杂技、传统美术、传统技艺、传统医药和民俗等领域。

Jiangxi boasts 88 national-level intangible cultural heritage items, 560 provincial-level representative intangible cultural heritage projects, 69 national-level intangible cultural heritage inheritors, and over 7,000 intangible cultural heritage practitioners at various levels, spanning fields including folk literature, traditional music, dance, theater, quyi (vernacular performing arts), traditional sports, acrobatics, fine arts, craftsmanship, traditional medicine, and folk customs.

近年来,江西通过"非遗+旅游"融合发展,打造了一批手工艺、美食、戏曲主题街区和场馆。一个个古老的江西非遗,正焕发迷人光彩。

In recent years, Jiangxi has pioneered "intangible cultural heritage+tourism" synergistic development, creating themed districts and venues dedicated to handicrafts, culinary arts, and opera. The ancient heritage items are now shining with renewed splendor.

兴国山歌

Xingguo Mountain Airs

　　兴国山歌是流传于兴国县及周边地区的汉族民歌,至今已有上千年历史,是客家人在劳作中消解疲劳不可或缺的工具。

　　Xingguo Mountain Airs are a genre of Han folk songs, originating in Xingguo County and its surrounding regions of Jiangxi Province, with a history spanning over a millennium. These ballads served as an indispensable tool for Hakka people to alleviate fatigue during their arduous work.

　　兴国山歌生动活泼,生活气息浓郁,有独唱、对唱、三打铁、联唱、轮唱等形式。

兴国山歌最为显著特点是，每首歌开头一句"哎呀嘞"，具有强烈的音乐旋律感。

The ballads feature lively and vivid expressions deeply rooted in daily life, performed in forms such as solo singing, antiphonal duets, "three-iron strikes"(a call-and-response style), choral ensembles, and round singing. Their most distinctive trait is the opening exclamation "Aiya-lei!", a rhythmic invocation that imbues each song with a musical pulse.

当地优秀的民间歌手都有一个特殊的身份——跳觋师傅。兴国山歌与跳觋的结合印证了民间信仰在传统音乐传承中的核心作用。跳觋既是一种民俗、民间信仰，也是兴国山歌传承的载体之一。

Notably, many famous local folk singers hold a unique identity as "Tiaoxi masters". This fusion of Xingguo Mountain Airs with Tiaoxi rituals underscores the pivotal role of folk beliefs in preserving traditional music. Tiaoxi, a blend of ritual practice, folk faith, and cultural performance, serves as one of the carriers for the inheritance of Xingguo Mountain Airs.

南丰傩舞

Nanfeng Nuo Dance

南丰是江西傩舞之乡。南丰傩舞，始于汉初，兴于明清。

Nanfeng is renowned as the cradle of Nuo dance in Jiangxi. Nanfeng Nuo Dance Originated in the early Han Dynasty and flourished during the Ming and Qing dynasties.

南丰傩事一般在春节期间进行，主要有"跳竹马""跳傩""跳和合""跳狮子""跳八仙"，统称跳傩；形式上有单人舞、双人舞、三人舞、群舞等；内容上有傩仪、傩舞、傩戏等。表演时，皆戴面具。南丰跳傩的面具，内容丰富，总量逾180种。

Nanfeng Nuo rituals are traditionally performed during the Spring Festival, mainly including "Bamboo Horse Dance", "Nuo Exorcism Dance", "Harmony Dance", "Lion Dance", and "Eight Immortals Dance", collectively known as "Nuo Dance". These rituals unfold in diverse forms, including solos, duets, trios, and group dances. The content includes Nuo rites, Nuo dance, and Nuo opera. Performers always wear masks. The masks of Nanfeng Nuo Dance are rich in contents, with a total of over 180 types.

南丰傩舞作为"中国古代舞蹈活化石",以千年的仪式、面具与舞步,承载着赣鄱大地驱疫纳吉的集体记忆,而傩神的鼓点继续在乡野与现代文明的对话中回响。

As a "living fossil of ancient Chinese dance", Nanfeng Nuo Dance carries the collective memory of driving away the epidemic in the Ganpo region with thousands of years of rituals, masks, and dance steps. Today, the rhythmic drumbeats of the Nuo deities resonate as a dialogue between rural heritage and modern civilization.

南昌瓷板画

Nanchang Porcelain Painting

南昌瓷板画是将中国传统的绘画艺术与制瓷技艺巧妙结合的一种民间艺术。清末"珠山八友"之一邓碧珊开创瓷上肖像画领域,瓷板画自此开端。

Nanchang Porcelain Painting is a folk-art form that ingeniously blends traditional Chinese painting techniques with porcelain craftsmanship. Deng Bishan, one of the "Eight Friends of Zhushan" in the late Qing Dynasty, pioneered the genre of porcelain painting,marking the beginning of porcelain painting.

南昌瓷板画既继承了中国传统绘画的精华,又兼容了中国陶瓷艺术的特点,其静中有动、虚中寓实、笔触细腻、状物传神,且具有不褪色、耐潮湿、耐日晒等特点,受到海内外各界人士的好评,1915年获巴拿马国际博览会金奖,1984年获全国旅游工艺品纪念品评比优秀奖,近年来获中国工艺美术百花奖和第一、第二、第四届中国工艺美术大师精品博览会金奖等大奖。

This art form inherits the essence of traditional Chinese painting while integrating the unique characteristics of Chinese ceramic art. Its hallmarks include dynamic stillness, ethereal realism, meticulous brushwork, and lifelike representation, coupled with fade- resistant, moisture-proof, and sun-resistant qualities. Recognized globally for its craftsmanship, Nanchang porcelain paintings have earned: Gold Medal at the 1915 Panama International Exposition, Excellence Award at the 1984 National Tourism Crafts and Souvenirs Competition.In recent years, it has won China Arts and Crafts Hundred Flowers Award, and Gold Medals at the 1st,2nd, and 4th China Masters of Arts and Crafts Expositions.

瑞昌剪纸

Ruichang Jianzhi(Paper-Cutting)

在历史的长河中，瑞昌剪纸如同一颗明珠，在千百年的岁月中熠熠生辉。考古发现，瑞昌剪纸的纹样风格，与当地汉晋古墓的出土文物的纹饰风格几乎一致。因此，瑞昌剪纸的起源极有可能追溯到汉代。

Through the annals of history, Ruichang Jianzhi (paper-cutting) shines like a luminous pearl, its radiance enduring for millennia. Archaeological discoveries reveal that the motifs and styles of Ruichang's paper-cuts mirror those of unearthed artifacts from local Han and Jin Dynasty tombs, suggesting a potential origin dating back to the Han dynasty.

瑞昌剪纸简练优美、构图匀称、造型生动、剪法明快，从起稿、剪刻、揭离，到粘贴、精修、定样，六大步骤，每一步都凝聚匠心与耐心。剪刀在手艺人的指尖下跃动，一套动作如行云流水，一气呵成。无论是门笺、礼笺，还是喜花、祭花，瑞昌剪纸，成为寻常百姓家的记忆。

Renowned for its elegant simplicity, balanced composition, vivid imagery, and rhythmic precision, Ruichang Paper-cutting follows six meticulous steps: drafting, carving, separation, pasting, refining, and finalizing. Each stage demands artisanal ingenuity and unwavering patience, as scissors glide through paper with fluid grace, transforming blank sheets into intricate masterpieces in a single, seamless motion. Whether adorning doorways, ceremonial scrolls, wedding decorations, or ritual offerings, Ruichang Paper-cutting has become the collective memory of ordinary households.

文港毛笔

Wengang Writing Brush

进贤文港镇位于江西抚河下游东岸，是北宋宰相、著名词人晏殊的故里。

Wengang Town, located on the eastern bank of the Fu River's lower reaches in Jiangxi Province, is the hometown of Yan Shu, a prime minister of the Northern Song Dynasty and renowned lyricist.

文港毛笔制作器具有 30 多种，制作原料主要为优质山羊毛、山兔毛、黄狼尾毛、香狸子毛以及植物竹等，制作工序有 126 道，主要分为芯毛制作、护毛制作、草灰制作、笔杆制作及芯杆组合、治笔、包装制作等六大工序。每一道工序又可细分为众多小工序。

The making of Wengang writing brushes employs over 30 specialized tools and relies on premium materials such as fine mountain goat hair, hare's fur, weasel tail hair, muskrat hair, and bamboo. The production process involves 126 meticulous steps, cate-

gorized into six major stages: core hair preparation, guard hair preparation, ash-binder processing, brush handle crafting, core-handle assembly, brush finishing and packaging. Each stage is further subdivided into numerous sub-procedures.

文港毛笔品种繁多,笔类齐全,式样新颖。近年来制作的"纯净紫毫""七紫三羊""墨翰"等品牌产品,名扬日本、新加坡等国家。

Wengang writing brushes are renowned for their diverse varieties, comprehensive brush types, and innovative designs. Recent brand pruducts,such as "Pure Purple Writing Brush", "Seven-Purple Three-Goat",and"Ink Elegance",have gained international acclaim,particularly in Japan and Singapore.

铅山连四纸

Yanshan Liansi Paper

铅山连四纸以毛竹为原料，纯手工完成多道复杂工序，"片纸不易得，措手七十二"是其生动描写。宋元时，铅山造纸已声名远播，明时铅山成为造纸重要基地，清中期纸业人口占全县十之三四。

Yanshan Liansi Paper is crafted from moso bamboo through a multi-stage, entirely handmade process. This labor-intensive tradition can be epitomized by the local adage: "A single sheet is hard to obtain; seventy-two meticulous steps are required." During the Song and Yuan dynasties, Yanshan's papermaking reputation spread far and wide, becoming a national papermaking hub in the Ming dynasty. By the mid-Qing era, nearly 30%–40% of Yanshan's population was engaged in the industry.

铅山连四纸具有纸质洁白、细嫩绵密、平整柔韧、防虫耐热、永不变色等特点，享有"寿纸千年"之美誉。明高濂《遵生八笺》赞其"妍妙辉光，皆世称也"，明宋应星《天工开物》亦多处记载铅山造纸状况，并给予很高评价。

Renowned for its snow-white luster, velvety texture, smooth resilience, moth-proof durability, and fade-resistant permanence, Yanshan Liansi Paper earned the reputation of "Millennium-Enduring Paper". Ming-era scholar Gao Lian praised it in *Zun Sheng Ba Jian* as "exquisite and radiant, universally acclaimed," while Song Yingxing's *Exploitation of the Works of Nature*(天工开物) documented Yanshan's papermaking techniques in detail, bestowing high accolades for its craftsmanship and quality.

乐平古戏台

Leping Ancient Opera Stage

古戏台营造主要包括选址、开工、制图、选料、施工等工序,建造和装饰采古典牌楼式样,由下部宽大台基、中部墙柱结构和上部巍峨屋顶三部合成,形成庑殿厅堂立面形象,构筑奇巧复杂、装饰豪华艳丽。

The construction of ancient opera stages in Leping encompass a meticulous process involving site selection, starting of construction, architectural drafting, material selection, and construction. These Stages adopt the classical archway-style (牌楼), integrating three architectural tiers: a broad stylobate in the lower part, a framework of pillars and walls in the middle, a towering roof in the upper part. This tripartite design evokes the imperial-style hip-and-gable roofline. The structure is exquisite and complex, and the decoration is luxurious and gorgeous.

乐平有记载的古戏台最早见于明代,现存明清以来的古戏台480余座,是目前国内古戏台保存最多最完好的县级市,享有"中国古戏台之乡"的美誉,堪称"中国古戏台博物馆"。

Historical records indicate that the earliest Leping opera stage was first seen in the Ming dynasty. Today, the city preserves over 480 opera stages of Ming and Qing dynasties.Leping is the county-level city that has the largest and best-preserved collection in China ,earning the reputation of"Hometown of Ancient Chinese Opera Stages"and the title of a "living museum of China's ancient opera stages."

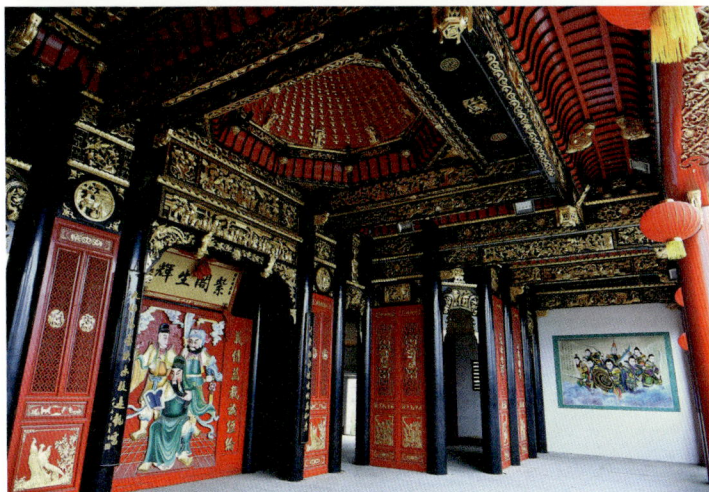

江西小炒
Jiangxi Stir-Fries

舌尖上的活色生香
Vivid Flavors on the Tip of the Tongue: A Sensory Symphony of Culinary Vitality

　　赣菜，又称江西菜，是中国传统八大菜系之一，以其独特的风味和深厚的文化底蕴，成为中华饮食文化中的重要组成部分。

Gan Cai, also known as Jiangxi Cuisine, ranks among China's Eight Great Culinary Traditions, celebrated for its distinctive flavors and profound cultural heritage, forming a vital thread in the tapestry of Chinese gastronomic civilization.

　　赣菜以鲜辣香醇著称，以鲜辣为主，辣中带香，香中透鲜，令人回味无穷。此外，赣菜还注重烹饪技法的多样性，如炖、煮、蒸、炒、烧等，使菜肴口感丰富，层次分明。

Gan Cai is renowned for its fresh, spicy, tasty and mellow flavors, with a predominant emphasis on freshness and spiciness, leaving a lingering and unforgettable aftertaste. In addition, Gan Cuisine places great importance on the diversity of cooking techniques, such as stewing, boiling, steaming, stir-frying, and braising, endowing the dishes with a rich and multi-layered texture.

赣菜"十大名菜"
10 Most Popular Dishes in jiangxi

    宁都三杯鸡、莲花血鸭、四星望月、余干辣椒炒肉、井冈烟笋、白浇雄鱼头、鳜鱼煮粉、甲鱼粉皮、藜蒿炒腊肉、滋补泰和乌鸡。

Ningdu Three-Cup Chicken(宁都三杯鸡)

Lianhua Blood Duck(莲花血鸭)

Four-Star Gazing the Moon(四星望月)

Yugan Chili-Stirred Pork(余干辣椒炒肉)

Jinggang Mountain Smoked Bamboo Shoots(井冈烟笋)

Steamed Variegated Carp Head with White Sauce(白浇雄鱼头)

Mandarin Fish with Fine Rice Noodles(鳜鱼煮粉)

Soft-Shelled Turtle with Sheet Jelly(甲鱼粉皮)

Artemisia Selengensis Stir-Fried with Preserved Pork(藜蒿炒腊肉)

Nourishing Taihe Silkie Chicken Soup(滋补泰和乌鸡)

江西"十大名小吃"
10 Most Popular Snacks in Jiangxi

　　瓦罐煨汤、南昌米粉、瑞金牛肉汤、弋阳年糕、九江萝卜饼、井冈糍粑、瑞州烧麦、碱水粑、黎川芋糍、安远三鲜粉。

Clay- Pot Simmered Soup(瓦罐煨汤)

Nanchang Rice Noodles(南昌米粉)

Ruijin Beef Soup(瑞金牛肉汤)

Yiyang New Year Cake(弋阳年糕)

Jiujiang Radish Cake(九江萝卜饼)

Jinggang Mountain Glutinous Rice Cake(井冈糍粑)

Ruizhou Siu Mai(瑞州烧麦)

Alkali-Water Rice Cake(碱水粑)

Lichuan Taro Dumplings(黎川芋糍)

Anyuan Noodles with Three Delicacies(安远三鲜粉)

第二部分

绿色

美丽江西

山清水秀

风景独好

Part Ⅱ
Green Jiangxi

Beautiful Jiangxi,
with Beautiful Mountains
and Clear Waters,
and Unique Scenery

江西的绿色生态画卷，以山水为底色，以人文为脉络，呈现出人与自然和谐共生的诗意栖居。这里山川秀美、江河如织、森林密布、鄱湖浩渺，"水清江豚跃""林深鹿饮溪""天净万鸟翔"已经成为美丽江西的生动名片。"江西山水真吾邦，白沙翠竹石底江"，北宋文豪苏东坡初到江西时，就创作了《江西》一诗，来表达他对江西山水的高度赞美。

Jiangxi's green ecological landscape, with its picturesque waters and mountains as the backdrop and cultural heritage as the connecting thread, embodies the harmonious coexistence of humans and nature in a poetic vision. The region boasts stunning mountains and rivers, dense forests, and the vast Poyang Lake. Scenes like "clear waters with leaping finless porpoises," "deer drinking from streams in deep forests," and "countless birds soaring in the clean sky" have become vivid symbols of beautiful Jiangxi. The literary giant Su Dongpo in the Northern Song dynasty, upon his first visit to Jiangxi, penned the poem "Jiangxi," expressing his high praise for the local scenery with lines such as "The mountains and waters of Jiangxi are truly my homeland, with white sands, emerald bamboos, and stony riverbeds."

　　庐山的云海松涛、井冈山的原始森林、三清山的奇峰怪石、龙虎山的丹霞地貌，共同构成"山峦叠翠、四时皆景"的生态屏障。境内鄱阳湖是中国最大的淡水湖、亚洲最大的候鸟越冬地、国际重要湿地，被誉为"珍禽王国""候鸟天堂"。全球98%以上的白鹤在鄱阳湖越冬，每年吸引着60万—70万只候鸟越冬栖息，湖面碧波与候鸟翩跹交织，演绎着生命与自然的交响曲。

The sea of clouds and pine waves on Mount Lu, the primeval forests on Jinggang Mountain, the strange peaks and rocks on Mount Sanqing, and the Danxia landforms on Longhu Mountain together form an ecological tapestry of "layered green mountains and scenic beauty all year round." Poyang Lake, located within Jiangxi, is China's largest freshwater lake, Asia's largest wintering ground for migratory birds, and an internationally important wetland, known as the "Kingdom of Rare Birds" and "Paradise for Migratory Birds." Over 98% of the world's white cranes winter at Poyang Lake, attracting 600, 000-700,000 migratory birds annually. The lake's green waves and the graceful flight of birds create a symphony of life and nature.

江西生态秀美、风景独好。"绿水青山就是金山银山。"绿色生态是江西最大财富、最大优势、最大品牌。全省森林覆盖率63.35%，活立木蓄积量7.10亿立方米，活立竹总株数26.86亿根，均位居全国前列，被誉为中国"最绿的省份"之一。

Jiangxi's ecological beauty is uniquely charming. "Clear waters and green mountains are invaluable assets." Its green ecology is Jiangxi's greatest wealth, advantage, and brand. The province has a forest coverage rate of 63.35%, a standing timber volume of 710 million cubic meters, and a total of 2.686 billion living bamboo plants, all ranking among the top in China, earning it the title of one of China's "greenest provinces."

江西是中国生物多样性最丰富的省份之一，已知有高等植物6337种，列入《国家重点保护野生植物名录》林业部门管理的有78种；已发现野生脊椎动物1007种，其中鸟类580种，约占全国的40%。鄱阳湖长江江豚约450头，占整个长江江豚种群近一半。

Jiangxi is one of China's most biodiverse provinces, with 6,337 known higher plant species, 78 of which are under the forestry department's management in the Catalogue of Key National Protected Wild Plants. A total of 1,007 wild vertebrate species have been discovered in the province, including 580 bird species, accounting for about 40% of the national total. There are around 450 Yangtze finless porpoises in the Poyang Lake, nearly half of the entire Yangtze finless porpoise population.

江西是中国首个绿色有机农产品示范基地试点省份，"生态鄱阳湖、绿色农产品"深入人心，"江西茶·香天下"香茗远播。作为首批国家生态文明试验区之一，江西为全球生态治理贡献了"江西方案"。

Jiangxi is China's first pilot province for green and organic agricultural product demonstration bases, with the concept of "Ecological Poyang Lake, Green Agricultural Products" being a household slogan, and the fragrant Jiangxi Tea renowned wide and far. As one of the first National Ecological Civilization Pilot Zones, Jiangxi has contributed the "Jiangxi Solution" to global ecological governance.

千山竞绿

Lush Mountains

踏遍青山人未老

Traveling through the Green Mountains, One Remains Youthful

从赣北的鄱阳湖平原到赣南的南岭余脉，山脉如巨龙蜿蜒，绿意如春潮涌动，各大名山尽展风姿，形成独特的生态资源矩阵。

From the Poyang Lake Plain in northern Jiangxi to the remaining ranges of the Nanling foothills in southern Jiangxi, mountains wind like giant dragons, and greenery surges like spring tides. Famous peaks such as Mount Lu, Mount Sanqing, and Longhu Mountain showcase their unique charm, forming a distinctive ecological resource matrix.

江西境内的庐山、三清山、龙虎山等名山，以其独特的自然风光和深厚的文化底蕴吸引着无数海内外游客前来观光旅游。习近平总书记赞誉"庐山天下悠、三清天下秀、龙虎天下绝"。

Famous peaks, like Mount Lu, Mount Sanqing, and Longhu Mountain, are renowned with their distinctive natural scenery and profound cultural heritage, attract countless tourists from home and abroad. General Secretary Xi Jinping has praised that "Mount Lu is the most serene, Sanqing is the most beautiful, and Longhu is unparalleled."

庐山
Mount Lu

庐山位于江西省北部九江境内。主峰汉阳峰，海拔1474米。庐山是一座历史悠久的文化名山，自古以"雄、奇、险、秀"闻名于世，享有"匡庐奇秀甲天下"之美誉。庐山被列为世界文化遗产、世界地质公园、中华十大名山、国家AAAAA级旅游景区。庐山拥有3000余种植物和2000余种动物，其垂直分布的亚热带常绿阔叶林至高山草甸带，堪称"天然植物基因库"。

Mount Lu, lies Jiujiang, northern Jiangxi province. Its main peak, Hanyang Peak, stands at 1,474 meters above sea level. It's a place of ancient cultural significance, known for being "majestic, wondrous, steepness, and picturesque," and is praised as "the most magnificent under the heaven." Mount Lu is a UNESCO World Cultural Heritage Site, a World Geopark, one of China's Top Ten Famous Mountains, and a national 5A-level tourist attraction. With over 3,000 plant species and 2,000 animal species, its vertical zones range from subtropical evergreen broad-leaved forests to alpine meadow, make it a "natural plant gene bank."

井冈山

Jinggang Mountain

　　井冈山位于江西省吉安市内，被誉为"中国革命的摇篮"和"中华人民共和国的奠基石"。90%的森林覆盖率孕育了南方红豆杉、银杏等珍稀物种，红色革命遗

址掩映于苍翠竹海中，红色文化与绿色生态在此交融。

Jinggang Mountain is situated in Ji'an City, Jiangxi Province. Hailed as the "cradle of the Chinese revolution" and the "cornerstone of the People's Republic of China," it carries profound historical significance. With a forest coverage rate of 90%, it nurtures rare species such as the southern Chinese yew and ginkgo biloba. Red revolutionary sites are nestled amid lush bamboo forests, where red culture and green ecology intertwine.

三清山

Mount Sanqing

三清山位于江西省上饶市东北部，因玉京、玉虚、玉华"三峰峻拔，如道教三清列坐其巅"而得名。主峰玉京峰海拔1819.9米。在1.5亿年雕琢的花岗岩峰林间，云豹、黄腹角雉穿梭于千年杜鹃花海，地质奇观与生物多样性相得益彰。

Mount Sanqing is located northeastern part of Shangrao City, Jiangxi Province. It gets its name from the three lofty peaks—Yujing, Yuxu, and Yuhua—which stand like the Three Pure Ones(Sanqing) of Taoism sitting atop their summits. The main peak, Yujing Peak, stands at an atitude of 1,819.9 meters. Shaped over 150 million years, its granite peak forests are home to cloud leopards and yellow-bellied tragopans that shuttle through seas of thousand-year-old azalea flowers. Its geological marvels and biodiversity complement each other perfectly.

龙虎山

Longhu Mountain

　　龙虎山位于江西省鹰潭市西南,是中国道教的发祥地、中国道教四大名山之一。东汉中叶,正一道创始人张道陵曾在此炼丹,传说"丹成而龙虎现",山因此得名。龙虎山是典型的丹霞地貌,有"丹霞仙境"之称。主要风景区有上清宫、天师府、龙虎山、仙岩水岩、岩墓群、象鼻山排衙石等。在丹崖碧水间,中华秋沙鸭在泸溪河畔嬉戏,道教祖庭与悬棺之谜为龙虎山生态景观注入人文厚度。

　　Longhu Mountain, is located in the southwest of Yingtan City, Jiangxi Province.It is the cradle of Taoism in China and one of the four renowened Taoist mountains in the country. In the middle of the Eastern Han Dynasty, Zhang Daoling, the founder of the Zhengyi School of Taoism, practiced alchemy here. Legend has it that once the elixir was completed, dragons and tigers emerged,giving the mountain its name.Longhu Mountain features a typical Danxia landform renowned as the "Danxia Fairyland." The main scenic spots include Shangqing Palace, Tianshi Mansion, Longhu Mountain, Xianyan Shuiyan, Rock Tomb Group, Xiangbi Mountain, Paiya Stone, and others.Here, Chinese

mergansers frolic in the Luxi River amidst red cliffs and clear waters. The ancestral court of Taoism and the mysteries of suspended coffins infuse the ecological landscape of Longhu Mountain with cultural deepth.

武功山

Wugong Mountain

　　武功山位于江西省中西部。当十万亩高山草甸随季风翻涌，夜空中萤火虫与星河辉映，露营者会惊叹"这是大地铺就的绿色银河"。自汉晋起，武功山被道佛两家择为修身养性之洞天福地，建起的庵、堂、寺、观达100多处，仰慕其名而登山游赏吟诗作赋的名人学士络绎不绝。

　　Wugong Mountain is located in the central-western part of Jiangxi Province. When the 100,000 mu (approximately 16,407 acres) Alpine Meadows surge with the monsoon, and fireflies in the night sky shine in harmony with the star-river, campers will exclaim, "This is a green Milky Way paved by the Earth!" Since the Han and Jin dynasties, Wugong Mountain has been regarded by Taoists and Buddhists as a blessed land for self-cultivation. Over 100 nunneries, halls, temples, and Taoist abbeys were built there. Celebrities and scholars have come in an endless stream to climb the mountain, enjoy the scenery, write poems, and compose odes.

此外，江西还有武夷山、明月山、军峰山等名山，它们不仅是地质奇观、地理坐标，更是生态智慧、绿色发展的时代答卷。井冈山的碳汇交易平台上，每片竹林的固碳量化作数字跳动；庐山植物园里，科学家用基因技术复活濒危的"庐山报春"……从山脉修复到产业转型，从碳汇交易到文旅振兴，这片土地用

行动证明:护住青山,自有金山;守住绿意,方得未来。

In addition, Jiangxi is home to other renowned mountains such as Wuyi Mountain, Mingyue Mountain, and Junfeng Mountain. These mountains are not only geological wonders and geographical markers but also embody ecological wisdom and respond to the call for green development in the contemporary era. On the carbon sequestration trading platform of Jinggang Mountain, the carbon sequestration of every bamboo forest is quantified into pulsating digital data. In the botanic garden of Mount Lu, scientists are using genetic technology to revive the endangered "Bellflower on Mount Lu."... From mountain restoration to industrial transformation, from carbon trading to the revitalization of cultural and tourism industries, this land demonstrates through action that protecting green mountains leads to wealth like gold mountains and safeguarding greenery ensures a bright future for the later generations.

万水皆清
Lucid Waters

波光潋滟入画来
Sparkling Ripples Alive in the Painting

赣鄱大地，以水为魂。自王勃登临滕王阁挥就"秋水共长天一色"，李白望庐山瀑布时泼墨"疑是银河落九天"，江西的水便成了流淌的诗行。

Water is taken as the soul of the land of Ganpo (Jiangxi). Ever since Wang Bo ascended Pavilion of Prince Teng and penned the line "The autumn water blends with endless blue sky," while Li Bai gazed at the waterfall on Mount Lu and penned the line "It seems as if the Milky Way were cascading from the heavens," the waters of Jiangxi has turned into the flowing verses.

五大水系汇鄱湖

Five River Systems Centered on Poyang Lake

　　江西是长江流域的重要省份之一，全省97.7%的面积属于长江流域，水资源比较丰富，多年平均降雨量1638毫米，多年平均水资源量1565亿立方米。境内河流、湖泊众多，全境10平方公里以上河流有3700多条，2平方公里以上湖泊有70余个。以鄱阳湖为核心，依托赣江、抚河、信江、修水、饶河五大水系，构建起独特的水网格局与生态屏障，其流域面积达16.2万平方公里，覆盖江西省97.2%的区域面积，成为长江中下游最重要的水源补给系统之一。

Jiangxi, one of the significant provinces in the Yangtze River basin, with 97.7% of its area belonging to the basin, boasts abundant water resources, with an average annual rainfall of 1,638 millimeters and an average water resource volume of 156.5 billion cubic meters. Jiangxi province boasts numerous rivers and lakes, with over 3,700 rivers larger than 10 square kilometers and more than 70 lakes larger than two square kilometers. Centered around the Poyang Lake, five major river systems (River Gan, River Fu, River Xin, River Xiu, and River Rao) constitute a unique water network and ecological barrier. The watershed spans 162,000 square kilometers, covering 97.2% of the territorial area in Jiangxi, making it a key water source rechange system for the middle and lower Yangtze River.

吞吐长江的水量调节器

A Water Level Regulator for the Yangtze River

　　鄱阳湖是中国第一大淡水湖，年均流入长江水量达1483亿立方米，约占长江流域年均径流量的15%，超过黄河、淮河、海河三河水资源总量。鄱阳湖如一方翠色砚台，纳尽五脉清流，又在长江洪旱季节发挥关键调蓄作用，以"洪水一片、枯水一线"的呼吸之态吞吐长江。春潮漫卷时，4125平方公里（高水位20米）的湖面烟波浩渺吞星月；冬寒水瘦日，仅500平方公里（低水位12米）的浅滩裸露如银链。

The Poyang Lake is the largest freshwater lake in China, with an average annual discharge of 148.3 billion cubic meters to the Yangtze River, accounting for approximately 15% of the river's annual runoff, surpassing the combined water resources of the three rivers (the Yellow River, the Huai River, and the Hai River). Like an emerald inkstone, the Poyang Lake gathers the five river systems' clear flows and plays a crucial role in regulating the Yangtze River floods and droughts, presenting a dynamic pattern of "a vest expanse in flood and a thin strip in drought", like the breathe of the river. Its water level fluctuates dramatically between flood and drought seasons. During spring floods, the lake expands to 4,125 square kilometers (at a high-water level of 20 meters), with vast waves swallowing stars and moon. In winter, when water is scarce, it shrinks to 500 square kilometers (at a low-water level of 12 meters), with shallow beaches exposed like silver chains.

诗画赣鄱
Pastoral Ganpo (Jiangxi)

风景这边独好

Unique Beautiful Scenery in Jiangxi

滕王阁的飞檐挑着千年月色,海昏侯国遗址诉说着大汉风华,望仙谷的崖壁灯火点亮仙侠幻境,春日油菜花海漫过婺源的青瓦白墙,白鹿洞书院的石阶刻满朱熹讲学的余音,景德镇的瓷韵是雨过天青翠欲流⋯⋯江西之美,美在绚丽多姿的山水生态,美在深厚的人文底蕴。

The upturned eaves of Pavilion of Prince Teng hold up the thousand-year-old moonlight, the ruins of the Haihun State tell of the grandeur of the Han dynasty, the cliff lights of Wangxian Valley illuminate a fairy-like fantasy realm, spring rapeseed flowers overflow the green-tiled, white-walled houses of Wuyuan(婺源), the stone steps of Bailudong Academy are etched with the echoes of Zhu Xi's teachings, and Jingdezhen's porcelain exudes a charm as refreshing as rain-washed celadon with vivid green hues. The beauty of Jiangxi lies in its splendid ecological landscapes and profound cultural heritage.

韩愈赞誉江西"江山多胜游"。江西是"红色摇篮、绿色家园",旅游资源十分丰富。全省现有世界遗产地5处(世界文化与自然双遗产地1处、世界自然遗产3处、世界文化遗产1处),世界地质公园4处,国际重要湿地2处,国家级风景名胜区18处。

Han Yu once praised Jiangxi as "a land of picturesque beauty". Jiangxi has been known as the cradle of revolution and a green homeland, abundant in tourism resources. Jiangxi province currently has 5 World Heritage Sites (1 mixed cultural and natural, 3

natural, and 1 cultural), 4 World Geoparks, 2 Ramsar Wetlands of International Importance, and 18 National Scenic Areas.

经过多年发展，江西现有旅游景区（点）2500余处。其中，国家AAAAA级景区15处，国家AAAA级景区213处。主要旅游景区可概括为："四大名山"——庐山、井冈山、三清山、龙虎山；"四个千年"——千年瓷都景德镇、千年名楼滕王阁、千年书院白鹿洞、千年古刹东林寺；"六个一"——一湖（鄱阳湖）、一村（婺源）、一海（庐山西海）、一峰（龟峰）、一道（小平小道）、一城（共青城）。

After years of development, Jiangxi now boasts over 2,500 tourist attractions, including fifteen national 5A-level and 213 4A-level sites. The main attractions can be summarized as: the "Four Famous Mountains"—Mount Lu, Jinggang Mountain, Mount Sanqing, and Longhu Mountain; the "Four Millennia Landmarks"—the ceramic capital of Jingdezhen, the famous Pavilion of Prince Teng, the academy of Bailudong, and the ancient temple of Donglin Temple; and the "Six Ones"—a lake (the Poyang Lake), a village (Wuyuan, 婺源), a sea (the West Sea of Mount Lu), a peak (the Turtle Peak), a path (the Xiaoping Trail), and a city (Gongqing City).

2024年12月，国家移民管理局发布了一条新政，新增21个过境免签人员入出境口岸，昌北国际机场纳入过境免签人员入出境口岸，南昌、景德镇纳入240小时过境免签人员停留活动区域。240小时就是10天时间，足够让一个外国游客在江西好好逛一圈，吃遍当地美食，体验中国文化了。

In December 2024, the National Immigration Administration (NIA)introduced a new policy, adding 21 visa-free entry ports, Changbei International Airport has been designated as an entry-exit port for visa-free transit travelers, while Nanchang and Jingdezhen have been included in the 240-hour visa-free transit zone for inbound tourists. This ten-day visa-free travel allows visitors ample time to explore Jiangxi, savor the local cuisines, and immerse themselves in Chinese culture.

江西精品旅游路线

Premium Tourism Routes in Jiangxi

红色旅游精品线路：南昌—井冈山—瑞金（兴国、于都）—安源。

Premium Red Tourism Route: Nanchang - Jinggang Mountain - Ruijin (Xingguo, Yudu) - Anyuan.

生态旅游精品线路：重点打造庐山、三清山、龙虎山、龟峰、铅山武夷山五个世界遗产品牌旅游产品和鄱阳湖国际湿地旅游。

Premium Ecotourism Route: Focus on crafting five world heritage tourism brands - Mount Lu, Mount Sanqing, Longhu Mountain, Turtle Peak, Wuyi Mountain in Yanshan, and the Poyang Lake International Wetland Tourism.

传统优秀文化精品线路：景德镇（陶瓷文化）—九江（世界文化遗产庐山、白鹿洞书院文化）—南昌（豫章文化）—吉安（庐陵文化）—赣州（客家文化）。

Premium Traditional Culture Tour Route: Jingdezhen (ceramic culture) - Jiujiang (World Cultural Heritage Site of Mount Lu, Bailudong Academy culture) - Nanchang (Yu Zhang culture) - Ji'an (Luling culture) - Ganzhou (Hakka culture).

绿色发展
Green Development

绿水青山就是金山银山
Clear Waters and Green Mountains
are Invaluable Assets

碧波荡漾,绿树成荫,山清水秀,江西省森林覆盖率位居全国第二,2024 年空气优良天数比率达 95.5%,2024 年地表水国考断面水质优良比例为 97.7%,县级及以上城市集中式饮用水水源水质达标率为 100%……这便是今日的江西。走进江西,宛若走进了一片绿色的"海洋",令人心旷神怡。

Jiangxi ranked the second in forest coverage rate in China, with shimmering waters, verdant trees, and picturesque landscapes. In 2024, the rate of days with excellent

and good air quality reached 95.5%, the excellent and good water quality rate of nationally monitored surface water assessment sections reached 97.7%, and the water quality compliance rate of centralized drinking water sources in county-level and above cities is 100%. This is Jiangxi today! Stepping into jiangxi,It is like entering a vast green "ocean", a place that refreshes and uplifts.

江西人民深谙"绿水青山就是金山银山"的智慧，通过立法保护自然生态，建立生态补偿机制，将环保意识融入日常生活。江西是中国唯一兼具国家生态文明试验区和生态产品价值实现机制国家试点的省份。近年来，江西坚定不移走生态优先、绿色发展之路，纵深推进国家生态文明试验区建设，积极探索生态文明制度改革，奋力打造国家生态文明建设高地，让美丽中国"江西样板"更有成色。

The people of Jiangxi deeply understand the wisdom that "Clear Waters and Green Mountains are Invaluable Assets", integrating environmental awareness into daily life through legislative protection of natural ecosystems and the establishment of ecological compensation mechanisms. Jiangxi has become the only province in China designated as both a National Ecological Civilization Pilot Zone and a National Pilot for the realization of ecological product value. In recent years, Jiangxi has unswervingly upheld the banner of green development, deepening the construction of the National Ecological Civilization Pilot Zone, actively exploring reforms in ecological civilization systems, and striving to forge a national ecological civilization highland, making the "Jiangxi Model" of beautiful China more vibrant.

首批国家生态文明试验区

One of the First National Ecological Civilization Pilot Zones

　　2014年，江西成为首批全境列入生态文明先行示范区建设的省份之一；2016年8月，江西获批成为首批国家生态文明试验区之一。经过多年改革试点，江西全流域生态保护补偿、山水林田湖草沙综合治理、生态产品价值实现等42项改革成果在全国推广，累计创建国家级"绿水青山就是金山银山"实践创新基地10个，绿色发展指数连续多年居中部地区第一位。

In 2014, Jiangxi became one of the first provinces to have the entire province included in national ecological civilization pilot demonstration zones. In August 2016, it was designated as one of the first national ecological civilization pilot zones. After years of reform, 42 innovations in Jiangxi, such as basin-wide ecological compensation, integrated management of mountains, waters, forests, farmlands, lakes, grasslands, deserts, and the realization of ecological product value, have been promoted nationwide. The province has established 10 national level bases under the concept of "Clear Waters and Green Mountains are Invaluable Assets" for ecological practice and innovation, and its green development index has remained first in Central China for many consecutive years.

"双碳"工作

Carbon Peaking and Carbon Neutrality Efforts

　　2024年,全省单位GDP能耗产出效益指数达到1.4,保持全国第一方阵。全

省可再生能源发电项目装机容量占全省总发电装机容量的55.2%。江西是全国首个实现设区市"国家森林城市"全覆盖的省份。

In 2024, the energy efficiency index per unit of GDP in Jiangxi reached 1.4, among the top performers nationwide. Renewable energy installed capacity accounted for 55.2% of the province's total power capacity. Jiangxi is also the first province in China whose prefecture-level cities are all designated as "National Forest Cities."

生态产品价值实现

Realization of Ecological Product Value

　　2019年9月,江西省抚州市成为全国第二个生态产品价值实现机制改革试点市。江西率先出台省级生态产品价值实现机制实施方案,择优在吉安、赣州、抚州3个设区市和11个县开展生态产品总值(GEP)核算试点,打造9个省级生态产品价值实现示范基地、14个示范基地创建单位。

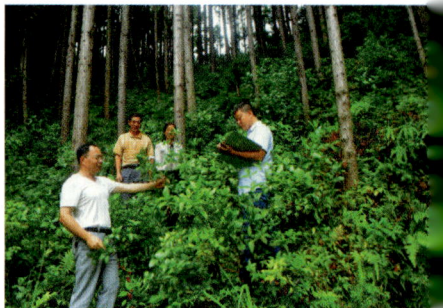

In September 2019, Fuzhou City of Jinagxi Province became the second national pilot city for the reform of the ecological product value realization mechanism. Jiangxi took the lead in issuing a provincial-level implementation plan for this mechanism, selecting three cities—Ji'an, Ganzhou, and Fuzhou—and 11 counties to launch pilots for the Gross Ecosystem Product (GEP) accounting and established 9 provincial-level demonstration bases for the realization of ecological product value and 14 bases for establishing model institutions.

生态补偿

Ecological Compensation

　　江西持续推进国家生态综合补偿试点省建设，推动实施多轮省内和跨省流域横向生态保护补偿，连续8年实施全流域生态补偿，累计发放资金近300亿元。

Jiangxi continues to advance its role as a national pilot province for comprehensive ecological compensation. It has implemented multiple rounds of intra-provincial and inter provincial river basin horizontal ecological protection compensation. Over the past eight years, Jiangxi province has consistently carried out basin-wide ecological compensation, with a total of nearly 30 billion yuan in funds disbursed.

第三部分

金色

金色赣鄱

产经引领

流光溢彩

Part Ⅲ
Golden Jinagxi
Prosperous
and Abundant
Ganpo(jiangxi)

中国东南腹地，有一片被群山环抱、江河滋养的沃土——江西。这里曾是古代海上丝绸之路的重要起点之一，新中国第一架飞机、第一辆柴油轮式拖拉机等都诞生于此。走进新时代，江西以独特的区位优势、优渥的生态资源和丰富的矿种资源，传承创新基因，接续奋斗，从"鱼米之乡"到"江西制造"，再到"江西智造"，持续擦亮"黄金枢纽""绿色矿藏""智造引擎"的金色名片，实现传统与新兴产业的"双翼共振"，向世界展露其磅礴崛起之势。

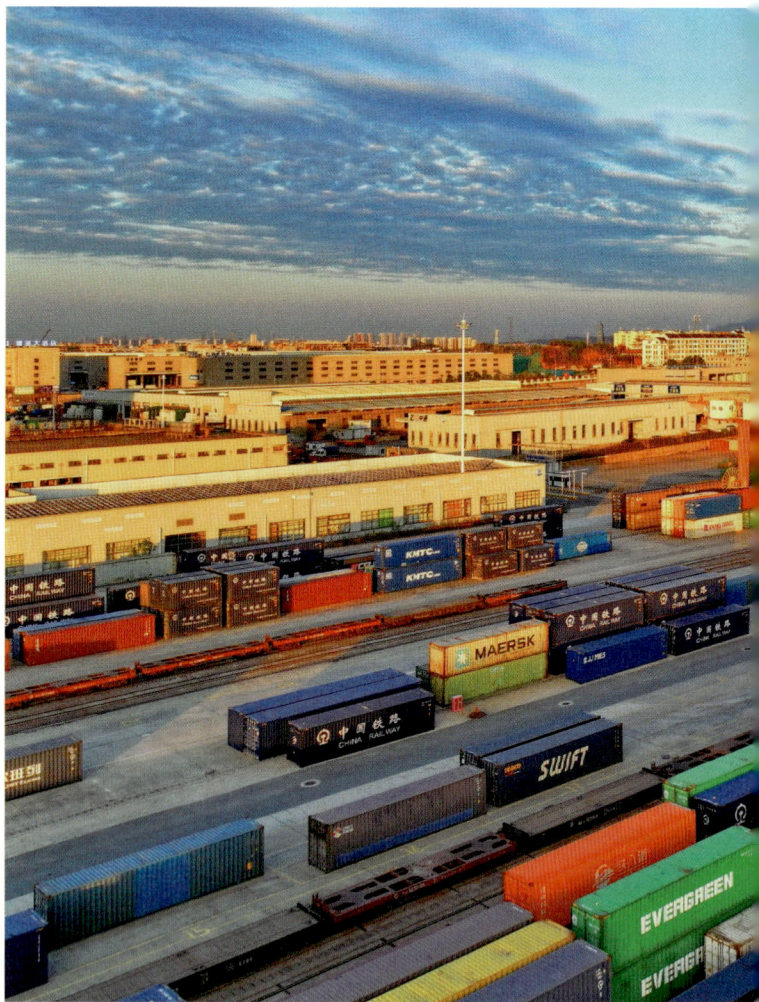

Nestled in the heart of southeastern China, surrounded by mountains and nourished by rivers, Jiangxi is a fertile land that was once one of the important starting points of the ancient Maritime Silk Road and the birthplace of People's Republic of China's first aircraft and diesel wheeled tractor. Jiangxi leverages its unique geographical advantages, abundant ecological resources, and rich mineral deposits to carry forward its innovative spirit. From the "Land of Fish and Rice" to "Jiangxi Manufacturing" and now "Jiangxi Intelligent Manufacturing", Jiangxi province continues to polish its golden name cards as a "Golden Hub," "Green Mineral Treasury," and "Intelligent Manufacturing Engine," achieving a "dual-wing resonance" between traditional and emerging industries and showcasing its momentum for a magnificent rise to the world.

区位优势
Location Advantages

通江达海的"黄金十字路口"
The "Golden Crossroads" Connecting Rivers and Seas

交通即机遇。金色赣鄱,首先在于其无可替代的地理枢纽地位。江西北倚长江,南接粤港澳,东连长三角,西通成渝经济圈,堪称中国版图的"黄金十字路口"。

Transportation means opportunities. The importance of Jiangxi lies first in its irreplaceable role as a geographical hub. Jiangxi is the "golden crossroads" on China's map for bordering the Yangtze River to the north, linking the Guangdong-Hong Kong-Macao Greater Bay Area to the south, connecting the Yangtze River Delta to the east, and extending to the Chengdu-Chongqing economic circle to the west.

随着昌赣高铁、赣深高铁等"八纵八横"骨干线路贯通,京九、沪昆、浙赣、皖赣、赣深等铁路干线在江西贯穿,江西已实现市市通高铁、县县通高速,与周边省份和沿海地区已构建了"空中1小时、高铁3小时、高速公路6小时"经济圈。

With the completion of key rail lines like the Nanchang-Ganzhou and Ganzhou-Shenzhen high-speed railways, part of the "Eight Vertical and Eight Horizontal" national transportation network, Jiangxi has achieved high-speed rail access for all its cities and

expressways for all its counties. It has built an economic zone with surrounding provinces and coastal regions, featuring "one-hour air travel, three-hour high-speed rail, and six-hour expressway" connectivity.

昌赣高铁、赣深高铁不仅缩短了江西与珠三角的时空距离，更成为"产业链黏合剂"，沿线新增7个百亿级产业集聚区，昔日的"交通洼地"已蜕变为"流动的金线网"。

The Nanchang-Ganzhou and Ganzhou-Shenzhen railways have not only shortened travel time between Jiangxi and the Pearl River Delta but also acted as "industrial chain adhesives," spawning seven new industrial clusters with output values exceeding 10 billion yuan along their routes. Jiangxi has transformed from a "transportation backwater" in the past into a "flowing golden network" today.

九江港的智能升级与"水铁联运"模式，让江西从长江"边缘港"跃升为华中物流枢纽。赣州国际陆港的中欧班列，则将稀土新材料送往全球新能源产业链的最前沿。这条"金色动脉"，不仅缝合了东西部经济断层，更让江西从"过路经济"的配角，跃升为辐射亚欧的产业枢纽。

The intelligent upgrade of Jiujiang Port and its "water-rail model" have elevated Jiangxi from a "peripheral port" along the Yangtze River to a logistics hub in central China. The China-Europe freight trains from Ganzhou International Port transport rare earth new materials to the forefront of the global new energy industry chain. This "golden artery" not only bridges the economic gap between eastern and western China but also elevates Jiangxi from a bystander in "transit economy" to a industrial hub influencing Asia and Europe.

2024年，江西省地区生产总值（GDP）达34202.5亿元。这一经济规模已接近或超过部分欧洲中等国家。在区域经济中，江西的规模可被视为东南亚中等经济体的"领头羊"。

In 2024, Jiangxi's GDP reached 3.42025 trillion yuan, a scale comparable to that of some medium-sized European countries. In terms of regional economy, Jiangxi stands as a "bellwether" among medium-sized economies in Southeast Asia.

资源禀赋
Resource Endowment

中国唯一"啥也不缺的省"
China's Only "All-inclusive" Province

　　江西矿产资源极其丰富,是中国最大的有色、稀有、稀土和铀矿产基地之一,素有"世界钨都""亚洲锂都""稀土王国"之称。特别是在战略资源领域,江西是中国战略资源的集大成者,甚至可以说是"啥也不缺的省"。江西已查明资源量的矿产就有153种,有80种保有资源量排全国前十,其中钨、钽、锂、铷、铯等14种矿产储量全国第一。铜、钨、铀、钽、稀土、金、银被誉为江西的"七朵金花"。

　　Jiangxi is exceptionally rich in mineral resources, serving as one of China's largest bases for non-ferrous metals, rare metals, rare earth, and uranium minerals. It is renowned as the "Tungsten Capital of the World", "Lithium Capital of Asia", and "Kingdom of Rare Earths." Especially in strategic resources, Jiangxi is a comprehensive repository—a province that "lacks nothing". There are 153 identified types of minerals in Jiangxi, with 80 ranking among the top 10 in reserves nationwide. Among these, 14 minerals, including tungsten, tantalum, lithium, rubidium, and cesium, rank first in reservation in China. Copper, tungsten, uranium, tantalum, rare earths, gold, and silver are hailed as the "Seven Golden Flowers" in Jiangxi.

宁德时代、比亚迪等产业巨头在此打造"矿山—电池—回收"闭环产业链，每吨锂矿资源价值提升10余倍，让江西成为全球锂电产业"金色心脏"。赣州稀土储量占全国三成，过去以"白菜价"外运原矿，如今依托中国科学院团队就地转化，稀土磁材价格翻升数倍，成为特斯拉电机、风电设备的"黄金原料"。

Industry giants like CATL and BYD have established closed-loop "mine to battery to recycling" industrial chains here, increasing the value of lithium resources more than tenfold and positioning Jiangxi as the "golden heart" of the global lithium battery industry. Ganzhou holds 30% of China's rare earth reserves. Once exported as raw ore at extremely low prices, these resources are now locally transformed with the help of teams from the Chinese Academy of Sciences, multiplying the value of rare earth magnetic materials and making them "gold raw materials" for Tesla motors and wind power equipment.

从"江西产"到"全球享"

From "Made in Jinagxi" to "Enjoyed Globally"

中医药产业:以"加速度"迈向全球舞台

Traditional Chinese Medicine Industry: Going Global with Acceleration

2024年6月27日,2024上海合作组织传统医学论坛在江西南昌举行,约600位与会中外嘉宾围绕"传承、创新、融合、发展"这一主题,交流互动、分享经验。截至目前,江西累计获批9个中医药领域国家级科技创新平台,101个省部级中医药科技支撑平台,中成药收入位居全国第三。以樟树和南昌中医药科创城为核心的产业集群,汇聚了仁和集团、江中药业等龙头企业,形成从种植、研发到流通的全产业链生态。

On June 27, 2024, the Shanghai Cooperation Organization Traditional Medicine Forum was held in Nanchang city,Jiangxi province, attracting around 600 Chinese and foreign scholars to exchange ideas on the theme of "inheritance, innovation, integration, and development". To date, Jiangxi has secured nine national-level Traditional Chinese Medicine scientific innovation platforms and 101 provincial and ministerial-level Traditional Chinese Medicine support platforms, with its Chinese medicine revenue ranking third in China. Centered around Zhangshu(樟树) and the Nanchang(南昌) Traditional Chinese Medicine Science and Innovation City, industrial clusters have gathered leading enterprises like Renhe Group(仁和集团) and Jiangzhong Pharmaceutical(江中药业), forming a full industrial chain ecosystem from cultivation, research&development to distribution.

江西有山野间蓬勃生长的草药,有工厂里精密运转的智能设备,更有传承千年的文化薪火。江西中医药产业,既是古老的,又是年轻的,既是中国的,更是世界的,正以开放姿态拥抱世界。

The Traditional Chinese Medicine industry in Jiangxi thrives with wild herbs growing in its mountains, precision intelligent equipment in its factories, and a cultural legacy spanning millennia. It is both ancient and youthful, Chinese yet global, embracing the world with open arms.

根据规划,到2025年,江西省将打造千亿级产业集群,推动中医药与旅游、康养融合,让世界游客在庐山脚下体验药膳,在梅岭深处探访智慧药园。

By 2025, Jiangxi plans to build a 100-billion-yuan industrial cluster, integrating Traditional Chinese Medicine with tourism and wellness, allowing global visitors to experience herbal cuisine at the foot of Mount Lu and explore smart herb gardens deep in the Meiling Mountains.

特色农业：对话世界的农耕文明

Specialty Agriculture: A Dialogue with the World's Agrarian Civilization

江西素有"鱼米之乡"的美誉，鄱阳湖的烟波浩渺与武夷山的云雾缭绕交织，孕育了茶香、鱼跃、橙甜的诗意农业生态。从千年茶韵到现代科技赋能，从湖鲜丰饶到柑橘飘香，江西正以开放的姿态，向世界递出一张充满生命力的农业名片。

Jiangxi is known as the "Land of Fish and Rice", woven with the misty waves of the Poyang Lake and the cloud-kissed peaks of the Wuyi Mountains that formed a poetic agricultural ecosystem consisting of tea fragrance, jumping fish, sweet tangerine. From millennia-old tea traditions to modern technology-empowered farming, from abundant lake delicacies to fragrant citrus fruits, Jiangxi is presenting the world with a vibrant agricultural name card.

茶产业

Tea Industry

　　江西不仅是茶叶的故乡，更是茶品牌整合的典范——江西从近700个分散品牌中，打造了以庐山云雾茶、狗牯脑茶、婺源绿茶、浮梁茶、宁红茶为代表的"四绿一红"五大品牌，每年投入亿元资金，推动茶产业向集约化、高端化转型。茶旅融合更是江西的创新之举：游客可在庐山脚下品云雾茶，在赣南茶园体验采制技艺，感受"茶香入梦，山水为伴"的东方生活美学。

Jiangxi is not only the homeland of tea but also a model of tea brand integration. From nearly 700 scattered brands, Jiangxi province has consolidated five flagship teas: Lushan Yunwu Green Tea, Gougunao Green Tea, Wuyuan Green Tea, Fuliang Green Tea, and Ninghong Black Tea, known as the "Four Greens and One Black". With annual investments exceeding 100 million yuan, Jiangxi is driving the tea industry toward intensive and high-end development. Tea tourism is an innovative highlight: visitors can savor Yunwu Tea at the foot of Mount Lu, experience tea-picking and processing techniques in southern Jiangxi's plantations and immerse themselves in the eastern aesthetics of "tea fragrance blending with dreams, accompanied by landscapes".

柑橘产业

Citrus Industry

　　江西是中国柑橘优势产区,是全国"赣南—湘南—桂北优质脐橙带"的核心区,柑橘栽培面积和产量均位居全国前列,形成了"赣南脐橙""南丰蜜橘""广丰马家柚""井冈蜜柚"等特色品牌。

Jiangxi is a leading citrus producer in China, forming the core of the "Southern Jiangxi- Southern Hunan-Northern Guangxi High-Quality Navel Orange Belt". Its citrus cultivation area and output rank among the highest nationwide, with brands like "Gannan Navel Orange," "Nanfeng Tangerine," "Guangfeng Majia Pomelo," and "Jinggang Pomelo".

油茶产业

Camellia Industry

　　江西是全球油茶产业的核心腹地，种植史可追溯至2300多年前。这片土地因气候温润、雨量充沛，被誉为"油茶生长的黄金地带"。2024年，全省油茶林总面积达1700万亩，茶油产能达44.2万吨，油茶产业总产值突破600亿元，油茶面积、产能、产值稳居全国第二。"江西山茶油"公用品牌以"东方橄榄油"之名惊艳世界，"赣南茶油"连续7年登上"中国地理标志产品区域品牌百强榜"，油茶产业成为赣南"绿水青山就是金山银山"的重要转化通道。

　　Jiangxi is the global heartland of camellia industry, with a cultivation history dating back to more than 2,300 years ago. Blessed with a mild climate and abundant rainfall, Jiangxi is hailed as the "golden zone for camellia growth". In 2024, its camellia forest area reached 17 million mu (11,333 square kilometers), with oil production up to 442,000 tons and industry output over 60 billion yuan. Its camellia area, output, and output value rank second in China. The "Jiangxi Camellia Oil" public brand has amazed the world as the "Oriental Olive Oil", while Gannan Camellia Oil has been listed as "Top 100 Regional Brands of Geographical Indication Products in China" for seven consecutive years. The camellia industry has become a vital transformation channel for the "Clear Waters and Green Mountains are Invaluable Assets" in southern Jiangxi.

现代服务业:以人为本,更好满足民生需求

Modern Services: People-Oriented,Better for Livelihood Needs

世界VR产业大会、中国景德镇国际陶瓷博览会、南昌飞行大会、樟树全国药材药品交易会、中国(赣州)家具产业博览会、江西国际麻纺博览会、江西国际移动物联网博览会等已发展成为展示江西的重要载体。2024年,全省服务业实现增加值17908.8亿元,比上年增长4.2%。

Jiangxi has been showcased by means of such key platforms like the World VR Industry Conference, China Jingdezhen International Ceramic Expo, Nanchang Aviation Expo, Zhangshu National Medicinal Materials and Drugs Trade Fair, China (Ganzhou) Furniture Expo, Jiangxi International Hemp Textile Expo, and Jiangxi International Mobile Internet of Things Expo. In 2024, Jiangxi province's service sector achieved an added value of 1.79088 trillion yuan, a year-on-year increase of 4.2%.

赣州市、宜春市、鹰潭市被列入全国首批城乡高效配送试点城市；南昌陆港型国家物流枢纽成功入选"十四五"首批国家物流枢纽建设名单；南昌市被列入全国第二批城乡高效配送专项行动实施城市。全省累计培育A级以上物流企业528家。

Ganzhou, Yichun, and Yingtan were listed among the first national pilot cities for efficient urban-rural distribution. Nanchang Land Port National Logistics Hub has been successfully selected as one of the first batch of national logistics hub construction lists during the 14th Five Year Plan period. Nanchang has been included in the second batch of cities in China to implement the special action plan for efficient urban-rural distribution. Jiangxi province has nurtured 385 logistics enterprises above A-level.

先进制造
Advanced Manufacturing

向世界递出科技创新的名片
Presenting the Business Card of Technological Innovation to the World

走进新时代，江西锚定新质生产力，以"黄金枢纽"的区位、"绿色矿藏"的禀赋和"智造引擎"的创新，向世界递出绿色与创新的名片——

In the new era, Jiangxi is anchoring new quality productive forces, leveraging its "golden hub" location, "green mineral treasury" resources, and "intelligent manufacturing engine" innovation to present the world with a name card of green development and creativity—

C919大飞机的机翼组件在南昌航空城诞生，让"江西造"飞向世界蓝天；

全球首个城市级量子通信网在赣州试运行,为数字经济筑牢"金盾";

盾构机"南昌造"不仅服务国内重大工程,更出口意大利参与铁路隧道建设,彰显"国之重器"的硬实力;

景德镇陶瓷借3D打印釉料和纳米抗菌技术重焕生机,青花瓷远销欧美;

南康家具集群引入AI大模型,木屑飞扬的车间蜕变为"共享智能备料中心"。

The wing components of the C919 airliner, born in Nanchang Aviation City, soar into the skies.

The world's first city-level quantum communication network is in trial operation in Ganzhou, building a "golden shield" for the digital economy.

"Made in Nanchang" tunnel boring machines serve major domestic projects and are exported to Italy for railway tunnel construction, showcasing the hard power of the key state assets.

Jingdezhen ceramics rejuvenate with 3D-printed glazes and nano antibacterial technology, and its blue and white porcelain is exported to Europe and America.

Nankang furniture clusters introduce AI models to transform sawdust-filled workshops into "shared intelligent material preparation centers".

Jiangxi is evolving from a "resource exporter" to a "value chain integrator," shifting from a geographical center to an economic hub.

江西从"资源输出者"到"价值链整合者",从地理C位逐渐向经济C位转变
——

Jiangxi is evolving from a "resource exporter" to a "value chain integrator," shifting from a geographical center to an economic one—

深入实施数字经济做优做强"一号发展工程",大力发展人工智能、VR、物联网等有竞争力的数字产业链群,在全国率先完成覆盖规模以上工业企业的数字化评价普查,获批建设数字化转型贯标试点省、"工业互联网+安全生产"试点省;

It is implementing the "No. 1 Development Project" to strengthen the digital economy, and vigorously developing competitive digital industrial chains like AI, VR, and IoT.It is the first in China to complete a digital evaluation census covering all large-scale industrial enterprises and has been approved as a pilot province for digital transformation standardization and "industrial internet + safety production."

布局"科学家+工程师+企业家+投资家"的未来产业联盟,建立科技成果"边研发、边转化"的产业化和快速迭代机制。

The province has Establish a future industry alliance consisting of scientists, engineers, entrepreneurs, and investors, and establish an industrialization and rapid iteration mechanism for scientific and technological achievements through simultaneous research and development and transformation.

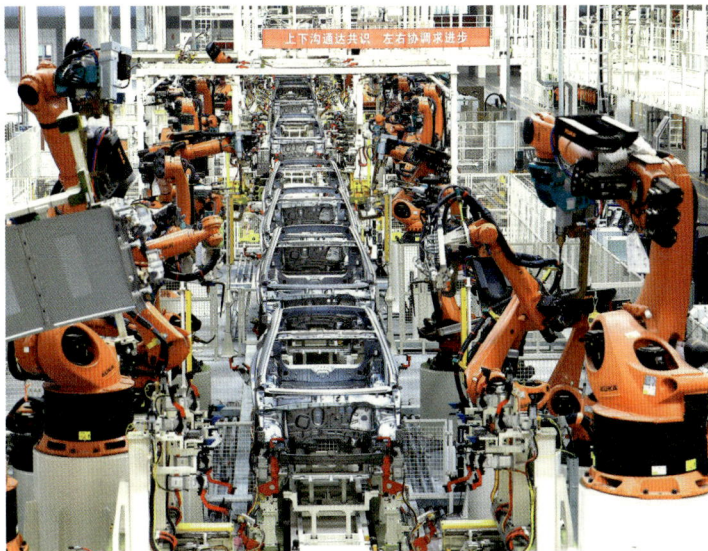

未来产业
Future Industries

布局新赛道，勾画新图景
Pioneering New Frontiers, Sketching New Visions

　　赣江畔的秋水广场，全息投影正勾勒出量子计算机的幽蓝光轨；景德镇陶溪川的星空市集里，3D打印陶瓷的机械臂与手工拉坯匠人比邻而居；赣州中国科学院稀土研究院的实验室中，指甲盖大小的永磁体正酝酿着新能源汽车的"心脏革命"……走进新时代，江西正在实施"1269"行动计划，打造12条千亿级产业链，电子信息、有色金属、新能源三大产业剑指万亿规模，航空、生物医药、量子科技等产业新星冉冉升起——

　　By River Gan, holographic projections outline the indigo tracks of quantum computers; at Jingdezhen Taoxichuan's starry market, 3D-printing robotic arms work side by side with hand-pulling artisans; in Ganzhou's Chinese Academy of Sciences Rare Earth Research Institute labs, thumbnail-sized permanent magnets are brewing a core revolution for new energy vehicles...Stepping into the new era, Jiangxi is implementing the "1269" Action Plan to build 12 100-trillion-yuan industrial chains. Three industries—elec-

tronics, non-ferrous metals, and new energy—are poised to reach trillion-yuan scale, while emerging stars like aviation, biomedicine, and quantum technology are on the rise.

空中雄心：南昌航空城为C919大飞机锻造机翼组件，景德镇航空小镇布局低空经济，无人机产业集群蓄势待发；

Aerial Ambitions: Nanchang Aviation City forges wing components for the C919; Jingdezhen Aviation Town layouts low-altitude economy; drone industry clusters are poised to take off.

数字新大陆：南昌VR产业基地产值占全国1/3，九龙湖元宇宙试验区打造虚实融合的"第二世界"；

Digital New Land: Nanchang's VR industrial base accounts for one-third of national output; Jiulonghu Metaverse Pilot Zone builds a virtual-real integrated "second world".

绿色革命：宜春锂电与宁德时代共建亚洲最大储能基地，赣州"中国稀金谷"将稀土磁材推向风电与新能源汽车产业链顶端。

Green Revolution: Yichun's lithium battery industry, partnering with CATL, constructs Asia's largest energy storage base; Ganzhou's "China Rare Earth Valley" pushes rare earth magnetic materials to the forefront of wind power and new energy vehicle chains.

每一个国家重大战略的出台，都会重塑全国的经济地理格局，再造区域竞争力。

长江经济带、中部地区崛起战略、景德镇国家陶瓷文化传承创新试验区、乡村振兴战略、赣南等原中央苏区振兴发展、赣江新区、长江中游城市群发展等,国家机遇叠加成网,进一步强化了江西的区位优势,也让江西经济强势崛起有了澎湃动能。

Every major national strategy reshapes China's economic geography and redefines regional competitiveness. Initiatives like the Yangtze River Economic Belt, the Rise of Central China Strategy, the Jingdezhen National Ceramic Culture Inheritance and Innovation Pilot Zone, Rural Revitalization, the Rejuvenation of Former Central Soviet Areas like Gannan, the Ganjiang New Area, and the Development of the Middle Reaches of the Yangtze River City Cluster have overlapped into a network, further amplifying Jiangxi's geographical advantages and fueling its robust economic rise.

江西"1269"行动计划谋划未来产业布局

三大赋能型产业

未来信息通信		未来新材料		未来新能源	
量子科技	工业互联网	稀土功能材料	石墨烯	氢能	新型储能

三大先导型产业

未来生产制造		未来交通		未来健康	
智能机器人	增材制造	永磁磁浮轨道	低空经济	基因编辑	智能诊疗

Jiiangxi's "1269" Action Plan for Future Industries

Three Enabling Industries

Future Information and Communication		Future Advanced Materials		Future New Energy	
Quantum Tech	Industrial IoT	Rare Earth Function Materials	Graphene	Hydrogen Energy	New Energy Storage

Three Pioneering Industries

Future Manufacturing		Future Transportation		Future Health	
Smart Robotics	Additive Manufacturing	Permanent Magnet Maglev Transit	Low-Altitude Economy	Gene Editing	Smart Diagnostics

第四部分

蓝色

心向蔚蓝

包容开放

交流互鉴

Part Ⅳ
Blue Jiangxi
Communication
and Mutual Learning

当景德镇瑶里古窑的千年火焰，穿越历史烟云，将青花瓷的温润与坚韧镌刻于世界文明的长卷，江西便已与"开放"二字结下不解之缘。

When the millennium-old flames of Jingdezhen's Yaoli ancient kilns pierced the mists of history, imprinting the warmth and resilience of blue and white porcelain onto the scrolls of world civilization, Jiangxi became inextricably linked with the word "openness."

因开放而兴的江西，向开放图强。从古代海上丝绸之路"瓷器外交"的辉煌篇章，到当代共建"一带一路"智能物流网络的壮阔征程；从鄱阳湖生态经济区绿色发展的勇敢探索，到赣江新区数字经济领域的迅猛发展——江西，这片古老而又焕发新生的红土地，正以国家级"试验田"的昂扬姿态，紧抓内陆开放型经济试验区建设的历史机遇，持续构筑内陆地区改革开放高地。

Prospering through opening-up, Jiangxi now strives for strength through opening-up. From the glorious chapter of "porcelain diplomacy" on the ancient Maritime Silk Road to the grand journey of jointly building smart logistics networks under the Belt and Road Initiative; from the bold exploration of green development in the Poyang Lake Eco-Economic Zone to the rapid rise of digital economy in the New District along River Gan, this ancient yet rejuvenated red land of Jiangxi is seizing the historic opportunity of building an inland open economy pilot zone, standing tall as a national "testing ground" continuously building a highland for reform and opening-up in inland regions.

一场广泛而深刻的变革，正悄然打破外界对江西"内陆即封闭""阿卡林省"的刻板印象。

A profound and sweeping transformation is quietly dispelling stereotypes of Jiangxi as a "landlocked and closed" Province or "Akalin Province".

国际贸易
International Trade

海阔扬帆正当时

Setting Sail on Vast Seas

对外贸易，作为江西开放型经济体系的坚固基石，是江西产品走向世界的主渠道，亦是江西参与国际产业分工合作的重要桥梁。

As the cornerstone of Jiangxi's open economy, foreign trade is the main channel for its products to reach the world and a vital bridge for its participation in international industrial division of labor and cooperation.

2025年3月,江西凯耀照明有限公司生产的12.5万只LED灯具,在九江港城西港区集装箱码头整装待发,它们将远销波兰,成为该公司2025年以来第20批出口欧洲的LED灯具。

In March 2025, 125,000 LED lamps produced by Jiangxi Kaiyao Lighting Co., Ltd. awaited shipment at Jiujiang Port's Chengxi terminal, bound for Poland. This is the company's 20th batch exported to Europe in 2025.

九江港,作为长江黄金水道的关键节点,2025年前两个月,外贸集装箱吞吐量达到2.6万标箱,同比增长7.18%。这仅仅是江西外贸企业加速"出海"拓展国际市场的一个生动写照。

Jiujiang Port, a key node along the Yangtze golden waterway, handled 26,000 TEUs of foreign trade containers in the first two months of 2025, a 7.18% year-on-year increase. This is just one vivid example of Jiangxi's foreign trade enterprises accelerating their "voyage" into global markets.

目前,江西与世界228个国家和地区进行贸易往来,越来越多"江西造"扬帆出海。

Today, Jiangxi trades with 228 countries and regions, and more "Made in Jiangxi" products are sailing across the seas.

外贸主体结构优化
Optimized Structure of Foreign Trade Entities

2024年，全省进出口总额达到4707.5亿元，其中生产型企业进出口额为3703.5亿元，占外贸总值的比重由上年的67.5%提升至78.7%，占比位居全国前列、中部地区首位，彰显了外贸主体结构的持续优化。

The total import and export volume in Jiangxi reached 470.75 billion yuan, of which production-based enterprises accounted for 370.35 billion yuan, rising up from 67.5% in the previous year to 78.7% of the total in 2024. This proportion ranks among the highest nationwide and first in central China, reflecting continuous optimization of its foreign trade structure.

2024年以来，江西出台了一系列支持外贸促稳提质的政策措施，推动商务发展资金重点向生产型企业倾斜。同时，加大外贸企业培育力度，助力未开展外贸业务的企业实现外贸"零"的突破。此外，江西还组织了2000余家企业参加境内外重点展会，帮助企业积极开拓多元化国际市场。

Jiangxi has rolled out a series of policies to stabilize and enhance foreign trade since 2024, directing commercial development funds toward production-based enterprises. It has also intensified efforts to nurture new foreign trade players, helping previously non-exporting firms achieve breakthroughs in this sector. In addition, Jiangxi province has organized over 2,000 enterprises to participate in key domestic and international exhibitions, exploring more global markets.

进出口产品结构优化

Optimization of the Import-Export Product Structure

　　机电产品已成为江西出口的主力军，2024年占出口总额的60%，较上年提升8.6个百分点。同时，锂电池、LED灯具等高附加值产品的出口增长显著。以孚能科技（赣州）股份有限公司为例，作为中国首批实现三元软包动力电池量产的企业之一，其生产的锂电池被广泛应用于电动汽车、无人机等领域。2025年前两个月，该公司新研发的电池产品出口货值近3亿元，较去年同期增长超8倍。

Mechanical and electrical products dominate the exports in Jiangxi, accounting for 60% of the total in 2024, an 8.6-percentage-point increase compared to last year. Significant growth has become evident in high-value-added products like lithium batteries and LED lamps. Take Farasis Energy (Ganzhou) Co., Ltd. for example. As one of China's first manufacturers of ternary soft-pack power batteries, its lithium batteries were widely used in electric vehicles, drones and other equipment. In the first two months of 2025, the export value of its newly developed batteries increased more than eight-fold to nearly 300 million yuan compared to the same period last year.

物流降本增效

Logistics Cost Reduction and Efficiency Gains

　　赣州国际陆港首创"中欧班列+海外仓+数字关务"生态链,通过区块链电子锁与北斗定位系统,实现货物从装箱到送达波兰马拉舍维奇的全程可追溯,时效压缩至12天,成本较空运降低70%。九江港与上海港共建"组合港",通关时效从48小时缩短至6小时,单柜物流成本下降700元。铁海联运吞吐量突破32万标箱,其中光伏组件、锂电池等危险品运输占比超40%,危险品运输处理能力居长江中游首位。

Ganzhou International Port pioneered the "China-Europe Freight Train + Overseas Warehouse + Digital Customs" ecosystem, using block-chain e-locks and BeiDou Navigation Satellite System to enable end-to-end cargo tracking from loading to Malaszewicze, Poland. This cut transit time to 12 days and reduced costs by 70% compared to air freight. Jiujiang Port's "combined port" initiative with Shanghai Port slashed customs clearance from 48 hours to 6 hours and lowered logistics costs by 700 yuan per container. Rail-sea inter-modal transport exceeded 320,000 TEUs, with dangerous goods such as photovoltaic modules and lithium batteries accounting for over 40% of the total transport, the highest handling capacity along the middle reaches of the Yangtze River.

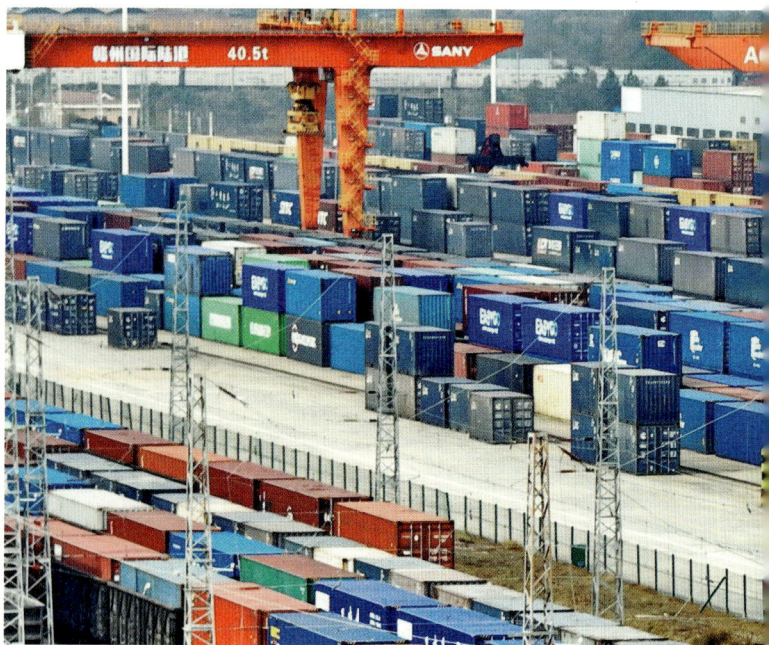

数字贸易催生新业态

New Business Models Driven by Digital Trade

景德镇"瓷宇宙"平台融合3D扫描、AI设计与区块链溯源技术，实现了"72小时数字制瓷"。2024年平台交易额突破15亿元，客单价提升至3.8万元。美国客商可通过VR设备实时参与青花瓷创作，景德镇匠人远程协作修改纹样，订单交付周期从90天缩短至15天。

Jingdezhen's "Porcelain Universe" platform integrates 3D scanning, AI design, and block-chain traceability to enable "72-hour digital porcelain production". In 2024, the platform's transaction volume surpassed 1.5 billion yuan, with average order values rising up to 38,000 yuan. U.S. buyers can use VR devices to co-create blue and white porcelain with Jingdezhen artisans in live engagement, shortening delivery cycles from 90 to 15 days.

对外投资
Overseas Investment

直挂云帆济沧海

Braving Winds and Waves with Full Sails

奔腾不息的赣江水，尽管百转千折，却毅然滔滔向海。在经济全球化的大舞台上，"江西面孔"愈发闪耀，展现出江西参与国际合作的热情、融入世界的智慧、坚定的信心以及强劲的动力。

Like the unyielding River Gan that winds its way to the sea, Jiangxi is making its mark on the globalized stage in international cooperation with passion, wisdom, confidence, and dynamism.

走出国门，方知市场有多大、前景有多广；走向世界，方能让江西融入世界、让世界瞩目江西；走上国际舞台，方可经略全球资源、助力江西发展。

Venturing abroad shows Jiangxi the boundless markets and prospects, engaging with the world enables it to integrate into global networks and draw global attention, while stepping into the international stage connects it with global resources to support its development.

"江西建造"助推"一带一路"互联互通

"Jiangxi Construction" Boosts Belt and Road Connectivity

江西对外承包工程以基础设施、能源开发、民生医疗、高端装备为核心领域，依托江西国际、江西中煤、中鼎国际等龙头企业，在共建"一带一路"中打造多个标杆项目。这些项目不仅提升了江西企业的国际市场份额，也推动了中国技术、标准的全球输出。

The overseas contracted projects of Jiangxi focus on infrastructure, energy development, livelihood and healthcare, and high-end equipment leveraging leading enterprises like Jiangxi International, Jiangxi Zhongmei, and Zhongding International. Flagship projects have been conducted under the Belt and Road Initiative, expanding its global market share and promoting Chinese technologies and standards.

在非洲北部，中鼎国际在阿尔及利亚承建的奥兰大学城项目，被当地媒体誉为"社会经济领域的一个卓越中心"。

In North Africa, the project of Oran University City in Algeria,undertaken by Zhongding International,was hailed by the local media as "an excellence center in socio-economic development".

在南亚，中铁九桥工程有限公司、中铁大桥局集团第五工程有限公司参与建设的孟加拉国帕德玛大桥项目，大大缓解了孟加拉河两岸民众的交通压力，架起了与共建"一带一路"国家的友谊桥梁。

In South Asia, the Padma Bridge in Bangladesh, built with contributions from China Railway No.9 Bridge Engineering Co., Ltd. and the Fifth Engineering Co., Ltd. of China Railway Bridge Bureau Group, has greatly eased cross-river traffic pressures and bridged friendships with countries jointly building the "the Belt and Road".

江西国际承建的赞比亚卢萨卡机场改扩建项目、江西久盛印尼东加电厂项目、江联重工埃塞俄比亚糖厂项目等一批投资超亿美元标志性项目，带动江西省装备、产品、技术和服务走出去，赢得当地业主和人民的隆重点赞。

Other landmark projects with investments exceeding 100 million US dollars, including Jiangxi International's Lusaka Airport upgrade and expansion in Zambia, Jiangxi Jiusheng's East Kalimantan power plant in Indonesia, and Jiangxi Lian Heavy Industry's sugar factory in Ethiopia, propelled the export of Jiangxi's equipment, products, technologies, and services while earning acclaim from local communities.

华坚鞋业埃塞俄比亚国际轻工业城、晶科能源马来西亚光伏产业园、柬埔寨西哈努克港园中园、白俄罗斯中白工业园建设植物盐项目等一大批劳动密集型制造业项目，有力解决了当地就业问题，又促进了江西省优势产业"走出去"和富余产能有效转移。

A host of labor-intensive manufacturing projects, including the Huajian Shoes Group's Ethiopia International Light Industrial City, the Jinko Solar's Malaysia Photovoltaic Industrial Park, the Sihanoukville Special Economic Zone Park-within-a-Park in Cambodia, and the plant salt project in the China-Belarus Industrial Park, have not only effectively created local job opportunities but also facilitated the "going global" of competitive industries and the efficient transfer of Jiangxi's surplus production capacity.

一组数据值得关注：2024年上半年，江西对外承包工程新签约合同10.3亿美元，同比增长316.7%。截至2024年7月，江西对外承包工程累计完成营业额15.6亿美元，国际化运营能力显著提升。

A set of notable data deserves attention: In the first half of 2024, the newly contracted overseas projects of Jiangxi amount to $1.03 billion, with a year-on-year growth of 316.7%. As of July 2024, the overseas contracted projects have achieved a cumulative turnover of $1.56 billion, reflecting a notable improvement in its international operational capabilities.

越来越多"江西路、江西桥、江西坝、江西井"等标志性工程扬名海外,"江西建造"成为江西参与共建"一带一路"的新名片。

More and more iconic projects, like "Jiangxi Roads", "Jiangxi Bridges", "Jiangxi Dams", and "Jiangxi Wells", have made "Jiangxi Construction" a new name card under the Belt and Road Initiative.

"江西援外"扩大国际影响力

Expansion of Global Impact via "Jiangxi Foreign Aid"

江西作为全国唯一承担两项中国政府援外农业示范工程建设（多哥农业技术示范中心、赤道几内亚示范农场）的省份，在西非打造了"中国大粮仓"。

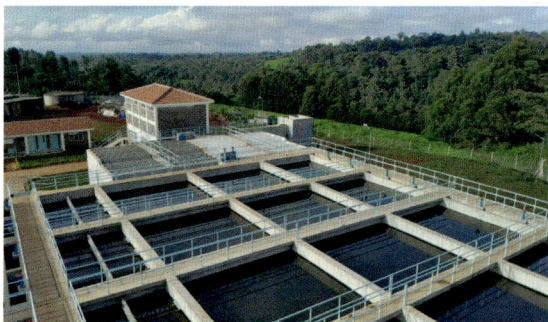

Jiangxi is the only province tasked with building two Chinese government-aided agricultural demonstration projects:the Togo Agricultural Technology Demonstration Center and the Equatorial Guinea Demonstration Farm, establishing"China's Granary"in West Africa.

近年来，江西企业秉承"实施一个项目、开拓一片市场、锻炼一支队伍、结下一份友谊"的理念，在亚洲、非洲、大洋洲等地区承建了一大批标志性援外工程项目。

In recent years, Jiangxi enterprises have adhered to the philosophy of "implement-

ing one project, opening up a new market, training a team, and forging a friendship." A host of flagship foreign aid projects have been undertaken by Jiangxi enterprises in regions across Asia, Africa, and Oceania.

这些援外项目注重民生与基础设施改善,通过技术输出和人才培养深化国际合作。例如,乍得供水项目直接惠及数万居民,蒙古口岸项目促进中蒙贸易额增长,莱索托消防项目填补当地公共安全短板。

These foreign aid projects prioritize the improvement of people's livelihoods and infrastructure, aiming to deepen international cooperation through technology transfer and talent cultivation. For instance, the Chad Water Supply Project has directly benefited tens of thousands of residents; the Mongolian Border Port Project has spurred the growth of trade volume between China and Mongolia; and the Lesotho Fire Protection Project has filled a gap in local public safety.

"江西援外"已成为江西省参与国际合作的新名片。

"Jiangxi Foreign Aid" has become a new name card for its engagement in international cooperation.

开放平台
Open Platforms

栽好梧桐引凤来

Planting Parasol Trees to Attract Phoenixes

    开放平台是对外开放的重要载体，也是改革创新的主阵地。近年来，江西开放平台的集聚作用更加凸显，开放通道更加畅通。

Open platforms are vital carriers for opening-up and key fronts for reform and innovation. In recent years, the agglomeration effect of Jiangxi's open platforms has become more prominent, creating smoother channels of opening-up.

    从政策支持上看，一个国家级新区、两个国家级试验区，改革开放的政策东风劲吹，江西迎来前所未有的发展机遇。

From the perspective of policy support, Jiangxi is embracing unprecedented development opportunities, driven by the tailwind of reform and opening-up. With one national-level new economic zone and two national pilot zones established, it has gained robust institutional momentum.

2016年6月，国务院批复同意设立江西赣江新区，这是中国第18个、中部地区第2个国家级新区，各项改革创新在这块国家级"试验田"上开花结果。

In June 2016, the State Council approved the establishment of the Ganjiang New Area of Jiangxi, China's 18th national-level new economic zone and the second national-level new economic zone in central China. Serving as a key testing ground for national reforms, this national-level platform has seen innovative activities take root and bear fruit.

2019年7月，景德镇国家陶瓷文化传承创新试验区获国务院批复，致力建设国家陶瓷文化保护传承创新基地、世界著名陶瓷文化旅游目的地、国际陶瓷文化交流合作交易中心。近年来，景德镇持续擦亮"千年瓷都"金字招牌，让"青花蓝"在海外绽放出新时代的璀璨光芒。

In July 2019, the State Council approved the establishment of the Jingdezhen National Ceramic Culture Inheritance and Innovation Pilot Zone. Designed to serve as a national base for ceramic culture preservation, inheritance, and innovation, this initiative also aims to develop a world-renowned ceramic culture tourism hub and an international center for ceramic cultural exchange, cooperation, and trade. In recent years, Jingdezhen has continued to enhance its prestigious title as the "Millennium Porcelain Capital," allowing the artistry of Blue and White porcelain to shine with renewed brilliance overseas, embodying the cultural vitality of the new era.

2020年4月，江西内陆开放型经济试验区经国务院批准设立，这是全国第3个、中部首个国家级内陆开放型经济试验区。近年来，"全国首创""中部第一""先行先试"的改革开放成果不断迸发，激发出经济发展的强大活力。

In April 2020, the State Council approved the establishment of the Jiangxi Inland Opening-up Economic Pilot Zone, China's third national-level inland opening-up economic pilot zone and the first in central China. In recent years, pioneering achievements in reform and opening-up, including "national firsts", "central China's inaugural pilot policies", and "groundbreaking trials", have proliferated across the region, unleashing great vitality for economic growth.

从重大经贸活动平台看,经贸唱戏越唱越"有戏"。江西省对接粤港澳大湾区经贸合作推介会、赣商大会、上海合作组织传统医学论坛、赣台经贸文化合作交流大会等重大活动成功举办。目标化清单化精准招商成效明显,12条重点产业链项目进资占招商引资实际到位资金比重超75%。

In terms of major economic and trade platforms, Jiangxi's "economic and trade performance" has gained increasing momentum. Successful major events have been held here, including the Jiangxi-Guangdong-Hong Kong-Macao Greater Bay Area (GBA) Economic and Trade Cooperation Promotion Conference, the Jiangxi Global Entrepreneurs Convention (GanShang Conference), the Shanghai Cooperation Organization (SCO) Traditional Medicine Forum, and the Jiangxi-Taiwan Economic, Trade, and Cultural Cooperation Exchange Conference, etc. The targeted, list-driven precision investment promotion strategy in Jiangxi has yielded remarkable results, with projects under its 12 key industrial chains accounting for over 75% of its actually paid-in investment.

从功能性平台看,开放功能越来越完善。江西获批国家级开发区19个,其中国家级经开区10个,国家级高新区9个;综合保税区4个,跨境电子商务综合试

验区9个，国家外贸转型升级基地12个，特殊商品指定监管场地6个，境外经贸合作区1个。

From the perspective of functional platforms, Jiangxi's opening-up-oriented infrastructure has been increasingly refined. It is home to 19 national-level development zones (10 national economic development zones and 9 national high-tech industrial development zones), 4 comprehensive bonded zones, 9 cross-border e-commerce comprehensive pilot zones, 12 national foreign trade transformation and upgrading bases, 6 designated inspection and supervision facilities for special commodities, and 1 overseas economic and trade cooperation zone.

越来越多的人看好江西、投资江西，内陆地区改革开放高地建设的前景更加广阔。

An increasing number of people are optimistic about Jiangxi and are investing in it, broadening the prospects for building the province into a highland of reform and opening-up in inland regions.

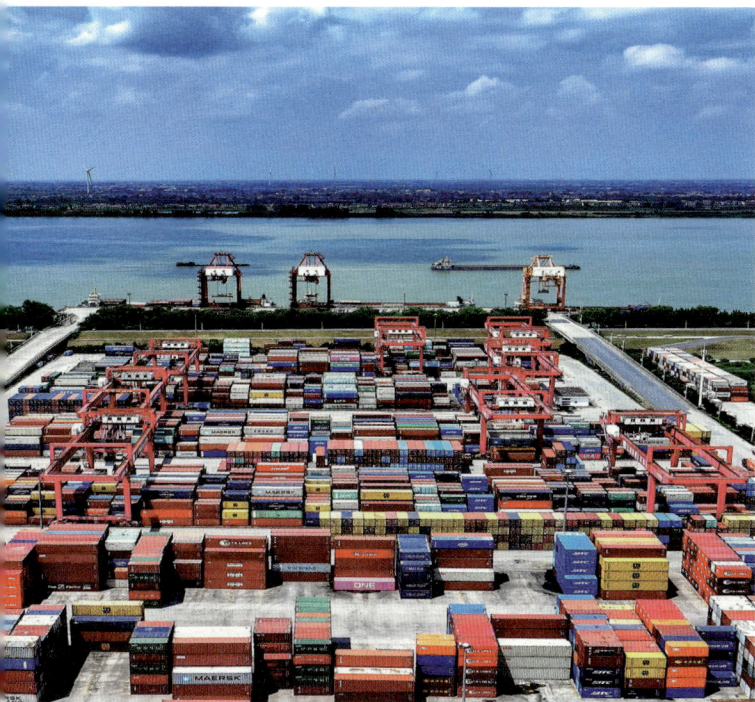

营商环境
Business Environment

春风化雨润商林

The Business Ecosystem Thrives under Nurturing Policies

　　营商环境是一个地区经济软实力和综合竞争力的集中体现,是稳定市场信心、激发经济发展活力、推动高质量发展的重要因素。

　　Business environment is the concentrated reflection of a region's economic soft power and comprehensive competitiveness. It serves as a crucial factor in stabilizing market confidence, stimulating economic vitality, and propelling high-quality development.

　　从国家层面看,2025年2月17日,习近平在民营企业座谈会上强调,民营经济发展前景广阔、大有可为,民营企业和民营企业家大显身手正当其时。这极大提振了广大民营企业和民营企业家的发展信心,预示着又一个充满希望的民营经济发展之春即将到来。

　　At the national level, the Private Enterprises Symposium was held on February 17, 2025. General Secretary Xi Jinping emphasized that private sector development has bright prospects and immense potential, and now it is the prime time for private enterprises and entrepreneurs to demonstrate their full capabilities. This has significantly boosted the confidence of private enterprises and entrepreneurs nationwide, heralding the arrival of a spring of hope and promise for private economy.

　　从省级层面看,2021年1月1日,《江西省优化营商环境条例》正式施行,为全省优化营商环境夯实了制度基础。4年来,江西紧抓优化营商环境"一号改革工程",为全省470多万经营主体的成长持续提供"阳光雨露""土壤养分",助力经

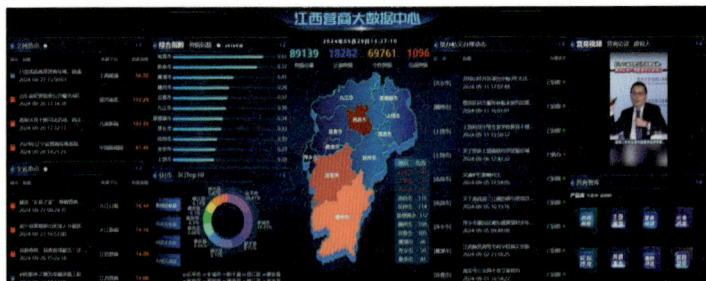

济发展行稳致远。

At the provincial level, *the Regulations on Optimizing the Business Environment in Jiangxi Province* officially came into effect on January 1st, 2021, laying a solid institutional foundation for province-wide business environment improvements. Over the past 4 years, Jiangxi has prioritized its "Flagship Reform Initiative" to refine the business environment, consistently providing "sunlight, rain, and fertile soil" to nurture the growth of over 4.7 million business entities across the province, thereby steadfastly advancing high-quality economic development.

政策筑基:以制度创新释放市场活力

Policy Foundation: Release Market Vitality Through Institutional Innovation

政策工具箱的持续扩容,为市场主体提供了"看得见"的安全感和"摸得着"的获得感。

The continuous expansion of the policy toolkit has endowed market entities with a sense of "visible" security and a sense of "tangible" benefits.

——构建"1+N"政策体系,推动政策红利直达市场主体。2024年,江西通过降本增效"30条"、助企纾困"28条"等政策累计为企业减负超353.9亿元。

—Jiangxi has established a "1+N" policy framework to facilitate the direct delivery of policy benefits to market entities. In 2024, thanks to the provincial initiatives like the "30 Measures for Cost Reduction and Efficiency Enhancement" and the "28 Measures to Support Enterprises in Overcoming Difficulties", over 35.39 billion yuan of costs have been reduced for enterprises.

——全面增强生产要素保障。截至2024年9月,江西制造业贷款余额达7942.97亿元,普惠型小微企业贷款余额突破9582.24亿元,为实体经济发展注入强劲动能。

—Comprehensive enhancement of guaranteeing factors of prodution. By September 2024, the outstanding balance of loans for Jiangxi's manufacturing sector reached 794.297 billion yuan, and the outstanding balance of inclusive loans for small and micro enterprises exceeded 958.224 billion yuan, injecting strong momentum into the development of the real economy.

——大力推进制度型开放。近年来,江西"高效办成一件事"改革全面深化,企业开办全流程一日办结率达95%,8个设区市实现开办零成本。房屋建筑类项目审批平均用时压缩至52天,招投标不见面开标率99%,低风险经营主体"无事不扰"率99.16%。

—Vigorously promote institutional opening-up. In recent years, Jiangxi has comprehensively deepened the reform of "streamlining the process to accomplish a task efficiently in one-stop service". The rate of completing the entire process of enterprise registration within one working day has reached 95%, and 8 cities with districts have achieved zero-cost business registration. The average time required for approval of housing construction projects has been reduced to 52 days, with a 99% rate of conducting bid openings without face-to-face interaction in tenders and bids. The rate of leaving low-risk business entities undisturbed unless there is a specific reason for intervention reached 99.16%.

法治护航:以公平透明构筑发展底线

The Rule of Law: Building the Bottom Line of Development with Fairness and Transparency

2025年1月,江西某乳业公司对媒体感慨:"谁能想到,两个月前,我们公司刚从破产重整中获得新生。"此前该公司深陷债务困境,濒临破产,江西法院系统创新破产审判机制,仅用3个月便完成公司重整,保留400余个就业岗位,成为"救治式破产"的典范。这只是江西推进营商环境法治化的零光片羽。

In January 2025, an executive of a dairy company in Jiangxi exclaimed in front of the media, "Who can imagine that we emerged from bankruptcy two months ago and restructured our company with renewed vitality". Previously mired in debt and on the brink of bankruptcy, the company was revitalized through Jiangxi's innovative rehabilitation-focused bankruptcy proceedings. It was restructured within three months, preserving over 400 job positions. This case exemplifies the "restorative bankruptcy model" for the whole province's enterprises, prioritizing enterprise recovery over liquidation. This is just one example of how Jiangxi is promoting the rule of law in improving its business environment.

江西推行"信用+双随机监管",对36.99万件案件实施"轻微免罚""首违不罚",释放执法温度。

Jiangxi has implemented the "Credit-Based Dual-Random Regulatory Mechanism", applied the policies of "exempting minor violations from penalties" and "not imposing penalties for first-time and minor offenses" to 369,900 cases, demonstrating the humane aspect of law enforcement.

新余市首创"商标+专利"混合质押融资模式,为赣锋锂业融资5.7亿元,开全省知识产权金融化先河。

Xinyu City pioneered the "Trademark & Patent" hybrid pledge financing model, securing 570 million yuan in funding for Ganfeng Lithium Group, a groundbreaking initiative that established Jiangxi's first intellectual property monetization framework at the provincial level.

在营商环境建设中,江西坚持"刀刃向内"的改革。法治化改革不仅规范市场秩序,更让"办事依法、遇事找法"成为企业共识。

In advancing its business ecosystem, Jiangxi has persisted in "self-targeted" reforms. Reforms towards the rule of law have not only standardized market order but also fostered a consensus among enterprises to handle matters in accordance with the law and seek legal solutions at times of difficulties.

服务提质:以数字赋能重塑政务生态

Service Quality Improvement: Reshaping Government Ecology with Digital Empowerment

政务服务从"能办"向"好办"跃升。数字政府建设成效初显,建成一批务实管用的基础设施和应用系统,安全保障体系初步构建,首批18项数字化标准体系和工作规范发布,数字底座支撑更加坚实。

Government services have achieved a leap from being "capable" to "user-friendly", marking the initial success of digital governance construction. A number of practical and effective infrastructure facilities and application systems have been established, a security maintenance system has been initially put in place, the first batch of 18 digital standard systems and operational specifications have been released, and the support from the digital foundation has become more robust.

以赣服通、赣政通、江西政务服务网为枢纽,打通多部门业务系统,将多部门办理的"单个事项"集成为企业和群众视角的"一件事"集成化办理,建立并联预审机制,实现省、市、县、乡四级窗口"一件事"一网通办。

Jiangxi has established an integrated governance framework anchored by its Ganfu Tong, Ganzheng Tong, and Jiangxi Government Service Network. By consolidating cross-departmental systems, the province transforms fragmented administrative procedures into user-centric "One-Stop Services" from enterprise and public perspectives. Through a parallel pre-approval mechanism, this system enables unified online processing of composite service packages across provincial-level, municipal-level, county-level, and town-

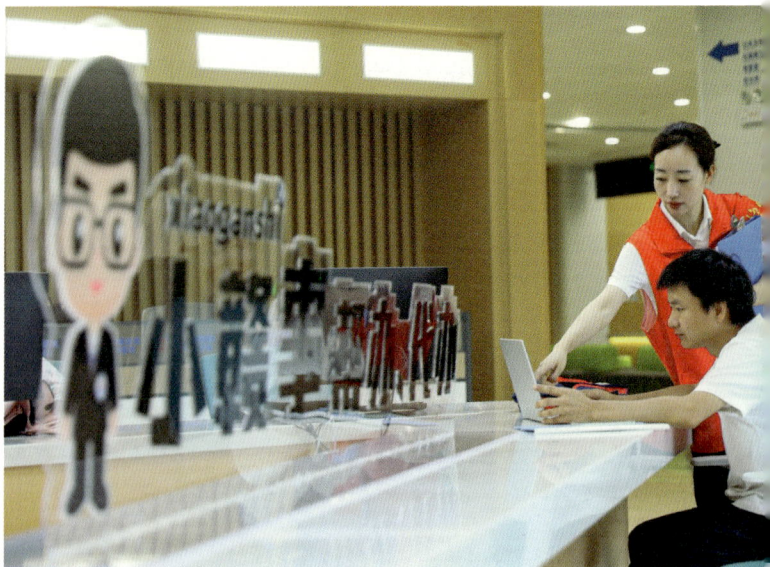

ship-level window services.

截至2024年底，涉及34个"一件事"的全省200余套办事系统全部被打通，受理部门实现高效协同、系统对接、数据共享。34个"一件事"平均办理时间从34个工作日压减为9个，办理环节从9个压减为2个，提交材料从14份压减为5份，企业和群众需跑动次数从5次压减为最多跑一次。

By the end of 2024, over 200 provincial-level service systems across 34 "One-Stop Service" systems had been fully interconnected, enabling efficient coordination among receiving departments, system integration, and data sharing. For these 34 "One-stop Service", the average processing time was reduced from 34 to 9 working days, the number of procedural steps decreased from 9 to 2, the number of required documents were cut from 14 to 5, and the number of required visits by enterprises and citizens was minimized from 5 to 1 at most.

拥抱全球:以国际标准推动改革创新

Embracing the World: Driving Innovation with International Standards

《江西省优化营商环境条例》实施以来,江西省累计出台对接国际标准的政策文件46项,在跨境投资准入、知识产权保护等18个领域实现突破。推出的"国际版营商环境20条",首次将外资企业设立"负面清单"压缩至28项,并在南昌、赣州试点"跨境服务贸易负面清单"管理模式。

Since the implementation of *the Regulations on Optimizing the Business Environment in Jiangxi Province*, Jiangxi province has rolled out 46 policy instruments aligned with global benchmarks, achieving breakthroughs across 18 domains including cross-border investment access and intellectual property protection. Notably, its "20 Measures for Optimizing the International Business Environment" marked a milestone by reducing the foreign investment negative list to 28 items and piloting a cross-border service trade "negative list" management model in Nanchang and Ganzhou.

南昌经开区试点QFLP(合格境外有限合伙人)制度,引入新加坡淡马锡资本设立50亿元新能源产业基金,带动韩国LG化学、日本东丽集团等跨国企业落地。

Nanchang Economic and Technological Development Zone piloted the QFLP (Qualified Foreign Limited Partner) system, attracting Singapore's Temasek Holding to establish a 5-billion-yuan new energy industry fund. This initiative has facilitated the establishment of regional operations by multinational corporations including Republic of Korea's LG Chem and Japan's Toray Industries.

赣州国际陆港创新"跨境贸易单一窗口"模式,整合海关、税务等8个部门数据,实现中欧班列货物通关时间压缩至1.5小时,较传统模式提速80%。该平台已覆盖"一带一路"沿线30个国家,2024年跨境电商进出口额突破120亿元。

Ganzhou International Land Port has pioneered the "Single Window for Cross-border Trade" model, integrating data from 8 departments including customs and taxation. This innovation has reduced customs clearance time for China-Europe Railway Express cargo to just 1.5 hours, an 80% improvement over traditional processes. The platform now connects with 30 countries under the Belt and Road Initiative, with cross-border e-commerce trade volume exceeding 12 billion yuan in 2024.

江西稳步扩大规则、规制、管理、标准等制度型开放,出台《关于深化投资贸易便利化改革的意见》20条举措,主动对接高标准国际经贸规则,为企业提供关税减让、贸易便利化等一站式服务；着力压缩通关时间，出口通关效率居全国第五、中部第一。

Jiangxi has steadily expanded its institutional opening-up across rules, regulatory frameworks, governance standards, and administrative protocols. It introduced 20 measures under *the Guidelines on Deepening Investment and Trade Facilitation Reforms*, proactively aligning with high-standard international economic and trade rules to provide enterprises with one-stop services covering tariff concessions, trade facilitation, and customs modernization. By prioritizing streamlined clearance processes, Jiangxi now ranks 5th nationally and 1st in central China for export clearance efficiency.

内陆开放型经济试验区建设取得新进展。江西至挪威奥斯陆、孟加拉国达卡全货运航线和跨境电商全货机专线开通，出口通关效率保持中部地区第一，昌北国际机场纳入过境免签人员入出境口岸，南昌、景德镇纳入240小时过境免签人员停留活动区域。

The construction of the inland open economic pilot zone has made new progress. All-cargo air routes have been launched, from Jiangxi to Oslo, Norway and Dhaka, Bangladesh, as well as dedicated cross-border e-commerce cargo flights. The export customs clearance efficiency in Jiangxi ranks first in central China. Changbei International Airport has been designated as an entry-exit port for visa-free transit travelers, while Nanchang and Jingdezhen have been included in the 240-hour visa-free transit zone for inbound tourists.

营商环境的优化转化为发展势能。2024年，江西地区生产总值增速连续三个季度保持中部第一，民营企业贡献率超68%。如，泰豪集团作为江西本土科技企业代表，在"民营经济31条"等政策支持下，近三年研发投入年均增长25%，成为江西智造出海标杆。全球锂电巨头赣锋锂业借助知识产权质押融资，实现纳斯达克上市，市值突破千亿元。

The optimization of the business environment has been translated into developmental momentum. In 2024, Jiangxi's GDP growth rate maintained its position as the fastest in central China for three consecutive quarters, with private enterprises contributing over 68% to this growth. For instance, Tellhow Group, a representative local technology enterprise, has seen its R&D investment grow by an average of 25% annually over the past three years under policies like the "31 Articles for Private Economy Development," becoming a model for Jiangxi's intelligent manufacturing exports. Global lithium giant Ganfeng Lithium leveraged intellectual property pledge financing to achieve a NASDAQ listing, with its market value exceeding 100 billion yuan.

赣江潮涌，江西营商环境不断迭代升级，必将为高质量发展注入更澎湃的动能。

As River Gan surges forward, Jiangxi's continuously improved business environment is poised to inject even greater momentum into its high-quality development.

对外交流
Foreign Exchanges

文明互鉴谱新篇

Exchanges among Civilizations Compose a New Chapter

文明越山海，一瓷跨千年。

Civilization journeys across mountains and seas; a single piece of porcelain boasts the histoury of a thousand years.

驼铃阵阵，羌笛悠扬；扬帆通海，乘风破浪。从宋代开始，景德镇瓷器就沿着古丝绸之路和海上丝绸之路源源不断走向世界，造就了"匠从八方来，器成天下走"的盛景。

Caravan bells resound, nomadic flutes croon; sails hoist toward oceans, vessels brave monsoon.Since the Song Dynasty, Jingdezhen porcelain has flowed ceaselessly along the ancient and maritime Silk Roads, craeting a prosperous scene of "artisans converged from eight directions, and masterpieces journeyed across the world".

如今的景德镇，每年都活跃着超过5000名"洋景漂"，他们汲取"千年瓷都"文化养分，用丰富多彩的艺术创作推动着中外陶瓷文化的融合与创新。景德镇陶溪川文创街区与意大利法恩扎国际陶瓷博物馆共建"数字瓷路"，运用元宇宙技术复原古代海上丝绸之路贸易场景，吸引86国青年线上体验，数字藏品交易额达3200万元。

Nowdays, Jingdezhen is home to over 5,000 international ceramic creators ("foreign Jingpiao" artists) annually. These creators draw inspiration from the city's millennium-old porcelain heritage, fostering cross-cultural fusion through innovative artistic practices. A landmark collaboration between Jingdezhen's Taoxichuan Cultural Creative District and Italy's International Museum of Ceramics in Faenza has builded the "Digital Porcelain Road". Leveraging metaverse technology, this project digitally reconstructs maritime Silk Road ceramic trade scenarios, engaging young people from 86 countries through immersive virtual experiences while generating 32 million yuan in digital collectible transactions.

时光回溯到400多年前，《牡丹亭》《邯郸记》《南柯记》《紫钗记》，"临川四梦"惊艳世人；《哈姆雷特》《奥赛罗》《仲夏夜之梦》《威尼斯商人》，世界四大悲喜剧让人魂牵梦萦。天各一方的汤显祖与莎士比亚各自创作出震惊世人的经典名篇，这恰是历史的巧合，也是文艺的幸事。

Over 400 years ago, the "Four Dream Plays of Tang Xianzu"—The Peony Pavilion, The Handan Dream, The Nanke Dream, and The Purple Hairpins—captivated the world with Tang Xianzu's genius. Simultaneously across continents, Shakespeare's four tragicomedies—Hamlet, Othello, A Midsummer Night's Dream, and The Merchant of Venice—leaving people with a lasting impression. Separated by geography, Tang and Shakespeare independently crafted works that staggered their respective worlds. This is a coincidence in history and a blessing in global literature and art.

400多年后，抚州举办新一届汤显祖国际戏剧交流月，以穿越时空、跨越国界的对话，架起人文交流的桥梁。赣剧《牡丹亭》融合全息投影与沉浸式剧场，在纽约林肯中心连演18场，90后观众占比达68%，《纽约时报》评价："让东方美学在数字时代重生。"

Four centuries later, Fuzhou launched a new Tang Xianzu International Theater Exchange Month, bridging cultural exchange through dialogues transcending time and borders. The Jiangxi Opera Peony Pavilion, fusing holographic projection with immersive theater, staged 18 consecutive performances at New York's Lincoln Center. Notably, the proportion of post-90s audience reached 68%. The New York Times acclaimed it as "reborn Eastern aesthetics for the digital age."

以文化人，才能凝结心灵；以艺通心，更易沟通世界。青春版《牡丹亭》，足迹遍布亚洲、美洲、欧洲的多个国家，热度经年不减。

Cultivating minds through culture fosters deeper connections; bridging hearts through art transcends borders more easily. The youth edition of The Peony Pavilion has traversed countries across Asia, the Americas, and Europe, maintaining its popularity over the years.

此外，江西与44个国家的114个地方政府建立了友城关系，江西企业在100多个国家和地区设立1000多家境外企业和机构，有212家世界500强企业在江西投资，对外经贸人文交流合作日益紧密。

In addition, Jiangxi has established twin-city relationships with 114 local governments across 44 countries. Meanwhile, Jiangxi enterprises have set up over 1,000 overseas enterprises and institutions in more than 100 countries and regions. The province now hosts 212 Fortune Global 500 companies, while its economic, trade, and cultural exchanges with the world continue to deepen.

又踏层峰望眼开。越来越多具备江西元素的优秀文化产品乘风而起、扬帆前行。中华优秀传统文化在传承和弘扬中日益彰显出旺盛强大的生命力、创造力、凝聚力、影响力。

We can ascend new heights where our vision broadens. Increasingly, exceptional cultural products infused with Jiangxi-style essence are greeting the winds of progress, sailing forward with ambition. Through inheritance and promotion, China's splendid traditional culture continues to reveal its boundless vitality, creativity, cohesion, and global influence.

当赣欧班列的汽笛声穿越里海，当非洲青年用江西技术烧制出第一窑彩陶……这片红土地上正在创造新的世界叙事。在这里，千年古窑的智慧与数字时代的锋芒碰撞，本土基因与全球视野共振。

When the Gan-Europe Freight Train's whistle echoes across the Caspian Sea; when African youths fire their maiden kiln with Jiangxi's ceramic technology... This crimson earth now weaves a new global narrative. Here, millennia-old kiln intelligence collides with the digital age's cutting edge, as native DNA resonates with global vision.

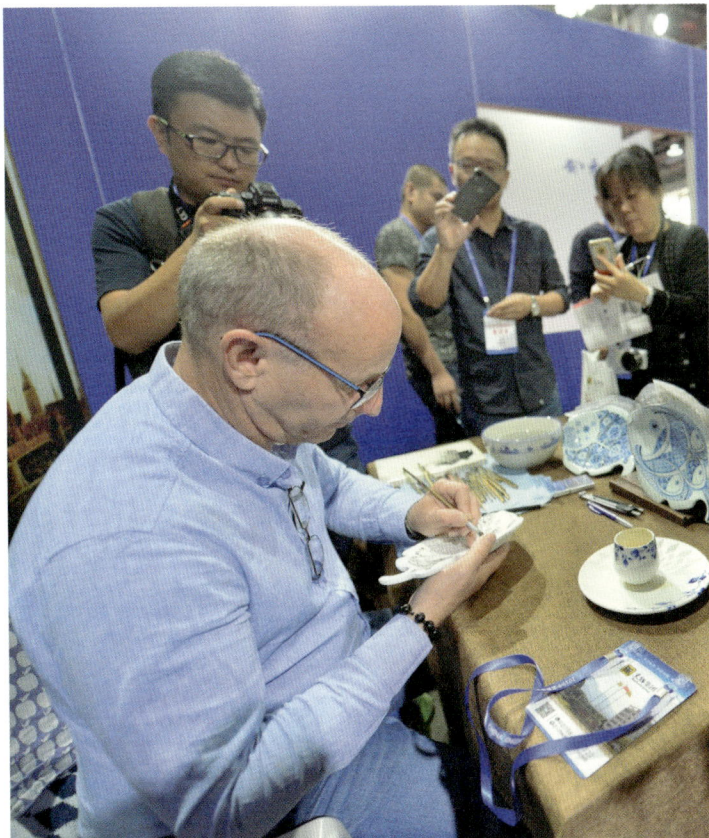

　　江西的故事，不仅是改革开放的微观样本，更是全球化进程中"和而不同"的生动实践。它向世界证明：真正的开放无关地理远近，而关于思想的高度、改革的深度、创新的锐度、合作的温度。这，或许就是"China"从瓷器走向未来的深层隐喻。

　　Jiangxi's story stands not merely as a microcosm of China's reform and opening-up, but as living testament to "harmony in divergence" in the process of globalization. It demonstrates to the world that true openness transcends geographical frontiers, manifesting through elevation of thought, profundity of reform, edge of innovation, and warmth of collaboration. Here lies the profound metaphor for China's journey from porcelain to futurity, where the ceramic soul that christened a civilization now fires the kiln of human destiny.

第五部分

红色

红土圣地

红色传承

红火生活

Part V
Red Jiangxi
Red Sacred Land
Red Inheritance
Flourishing Life

如果用一种颜色来描绘江西,那么最耀眼的颜色莫过于红色。

If we use one color to describe Jiangxi, the most dazzling color is undoubtedly red.

江西,是一片镌刻着信念与荣光的红色沃土,是中国革命的摇篮、人民军队的摇篮、共和国的摇篮、中国工人运动的策源地。这片土地上浸染着无数革命烈士的鲜血,孕育了伟大的井冈山精神、苏区精神、长征精神,承载着中国共产党人的初心使命。

Jiangxi stands as a revolutionary heartland etched with unwavering faith and historic glory. It is the cradle of the Chinese Revolution, the cradle of the Chinese People's Army, the cradle of the People's Republic, and the seminal hub of Chinese labor movement. This sacred land, steeped in the sacrifices of countless revolutionary martyrs, has given rise to enduring ideological legacies: the Spirit of Jinggang Mountains, the Spirit of Former Central Soviet Areas, and the Spirit of the Long March. These pillars collectively embody the founding aspirations and historic mission of the Communist Party of China (CPC).

土地革命战争时期,载入"革命烈士英名录"的江西革命烈士就有26万人,占全国的1/6,他们为中国革命胜利作出了重大贡献。

During the Agrarian Revolution War, Jiangxi Province documented 260, 000 revolutionary martyrs in the "National List of Revolutionary Martyrs", representing one-sixth of China's total martyrs and cementing its pivotal role in securing the ultimate triumph of the Chinese Revolution.

如今的赣鄱大地，红色基因代代相传，改革发展日新月异，放眼望去，处处都是活跃的创新创造，处处涌动着革故鼎新的澎湃浪潮。江西人民锐意进取、奋力前行，实现了从封闭落后向文明进步、从温饱不足向全面小康的历史性巨变，见证了中国共产党团结带领中国人民实现从站起来、富起来到强起来的伟大飞跃。

Today's Ganpo(Jiangxi) is a land deeply rooted in revolutionary heritage, and the spirit of reform pulses with unrelenting vitality. Vibrant innovation thrives across its cities and countryside, with the surging waves of transformation, serving as a testament to Jiangxi province's metamorphosis from an isolated, underdeveloped region into a civilization of progress and comprehensive moderate prosperity. Through tenacious advancement, the people of Jiangxi have scripted a historic saga from subsistence to abundance and from backwardness to modernity, mirroring the Chinese nation's epochal journey under CPC leadership of rising from adversity, prospering through reform, and ascending to global prominence.

凡是过往，皆为序章。党的十八大以来，习近平总书记三次赴江西考察，为江西发展把脉定向、指路引航，对江西寄予厚望。如今的江西，政通人和，百业俱兴，4500多万赣鄱儿女踔厉奋发，正在以新的姿态谱写中国式现代化江西篇章。

What's past is prologue. Since the 18th National Congress of the CPC, General Secretary Xi Jinping has made three inspection tours to Jiangxi to provide guidance and direction for the province's development, placing high expectations on this revolutionary heartland. Today's Jiangxi thrives with effective governance, social cohesion, and booming industries. Over 45 million determined people are forging ahead with renewed vigor, composing a Jiangxi chapter of Chinese modernization through concrete actions.

革命圣地　红色摇篮

Holy Land of the Revolution, Red Cradles

井冈山：中国革命的摇篮

Jinggang Mountain: The Cradle of Chinese Revolution

井冈山山高林密，层峦叠嶂，地势险峻。1927年秋，毛泽东、朱德等中国共产党人率领中国工农红军，在这里创建了第一个农村革命根据地，开辟了一条"农村包围城市，武装夺取政权"的革命新道路。井冈山以"中国革命的摇篮"而饮誉海内外。正是因为有着信仰的光辉、奋斗的史诗、人民的伟力，井冈山，这片被无数先烈染红的土地，成为中国革命的圣地。

Jinggang Mountain, with its towering peaks, dense forests, and rugged terrain, stands as a natural fortress. In the autumn of 1927, Mao Zedong, Zhu De, and other Chinese Communists led the Red Army of the Workers and Peasants of China to establish the first rural revolutionary base area here, pioneering a revolutionary path of "encircling the cities from the countryside and seizing state power through armed struggle." Jinggang Mountain is renowned worldwide as the "Cradle of the Chinese Revolution." It is precisely because of the radiance of faith, the epic of struggle, and the great power of the people that Jinggang Mountain, this land dyed red by the blood of countless martyrs, has become a sacred place of the Chinese revolution.

南昌：人民军队的摇篮

Nanchang: The Cradle of the People's army

    1927年8月1日，在南昌这座城市爆发了对后世影响深远的南昌起义。南昌起义打响了武装反抗国民党反动派的第一枪，标志着中国共产党独立领导革命战争和创建革命军队的开始。也正因如此，南昌被誉为"英雄城""军旗升起的地方""人民军队的摇篮"。

On August 1, 1927, the Nanchang Uprising erupted in this historic city, a watershed moment that reshaped China's revolutionary trajectory. This armed revolt, the first organized resistance against the Kuomintang regime, marked the inaugural step of the Communist Party of China (CPC) in independent military leadership and forging its revolutionary armed forces. Cementing its legacy, Nanchang is venerated as the "City of Heroes", "The place where the militray flag is raised",and "The place Where the People's Army Was Born".

瑞金：共和国的摇篮

Ruijin: The Cradle of the Republic

　　瑞金，是中华苏维埃共和国临时中央政府的诞生地，中央红军二万五千里长征出发地，被誉为"共和国的摇篮"。从1931年中华苏维埃共和国临时中央政府在瑞金宣告成立，到1934年红军长征，这片土地见证了无数革命者的热血与奋斗。"装点此关山，今朝更好看。"如今，这座承载着共和国基因的城市，正以开放包容的姿态，续写着红色血脉与时代发展的新篇章。

　　Ruijin is the birthplace of the Temporay Central Government of Chinese Soviet Republic and the starting point of the Central Red Army's 25,000-mile Long March, honored as the "Cradle of the People's Republic." From the proclamation of the Temporay Central Government of Chinese Soviet Republic in 1931 to the commencement of the Long March in 1934, this land bore witness to the fervor and struggles of countless revolutionaries. "Adorned with heroic deeds, these mountains and rivers now shine more brilliantly than ever." Today, this city carrying the genetic code of the People's Republic embraces a new chapter with open arms, weaving the legacy of revolutionary spirit into contemporary development.

安源：中国工人运动的策源地

Anyuan: The Birthplace of Chinese Labor Movement

安源，是中国工人运动的策源地、秋收起义的主要爆发地。毛泽东、刘少奇、李立三等革命家在此开展早期工运实践。在这里，中国共产党领导了安源路矿工人大罢工并取得胜利，开创了"全国产业工人中最早的党支部""全国最早的中共地方党校"等15个全国之最。"工人万岁！"第一次在这里传响世界。因此，安源也被誉为"东方的莫斯科"、中国革命早期"无产阶级的大本营"。

Anyuan is the birthplace of Chinese Labor Movement and a major theater of the Autumn Harvest Uprising, where it witnessed the early labor movement practices of revolutionaries like Mao Zedong, Liu Shaoqi, and Li Lisan. Here, the Communist Party of China led the Railway Workers' and Coal Miners' Movement in Anyuan to victory, establishing 15 pioneering initiatives including "China's earliest industrial worker party branch" and "the nation's first local CPC party school." It was in this land where the rallying cry "Long live the workers!" first echoed to the world, earning Anyuan the accolades of "Moscow of the East" and the "proletarian stronghold" in the early Chinese revolution.

红色传承
Red Heritage

红色基因代代相传

The Red Gene is Passed down from Generation to Generation

神山村

Village Shenshan

　　走在井冈山神山村的街道上，脚下是青石板路，周边耸立着一栋栋白墙褐瓦的客家民居，溪水潺潺流淌，让人仿佛置身文人墨客笔下的"梦里江南"。谁会想到，这里曾是个省定贫困村，全村54户231人中，曾有贫困户21户61人。正是在

这个小山村，习近平总书记对乡亲们说，我们党是全心全意为人民服务的党，将继续大力支持老区发展，让乡亲们日子越过越好。在扶贫的路上，不能落下一个贫困家庭、丢下一个贫困群众。

Walking along the streets of Village Shenshan in Jinggang Mountain, one treads on bluestone paths flanked by white-walled, brown-tiled Hakka-style houses, while murmuring streams evoke the idyllic Jiangnan region as depicted in classical Chinese literature. Few would imagine this picturesque settlement was once a designated poverty-stricken village at the provincial level, where 21 out of 54 households (61 individuals out of 231 people) languished in poverty. It was here that General Secretary Xi Jinping affirmed to the villagers: Our Party, which wholeheartedly serves the people, will continue to vigorously support development in old revolutionary base areas, ensuring everyone's lives keep improving. On the path of poverty alleviation, we must leave no family or individual behind.

华屋村

Village Huawu

　　赣闽交界的瑞金市叶坪乡有一个华屋村,村后山的蛤蟆岭上,有十七棵昂然挺立的青松,人们称之为"信念树"。1934年,红军北上长征,17名华屋村儿郎与亲人告别,临行前在后山种下了17棵青松。战士们深知,参加革命就意味着可能会牺牲,栽下松树,就是坚信:"青松常在,革命必胜!"华屋村17儿郎北上无音讯,最后全部壮烈牺牲。青松依旧在,浩气留人间!

In Village Huawu, Yeping Township, Ruijin City, where the borders of Jiangxi and Fujian provinces meet, stands a legendary landmark on Toad Ridge behind the village—17 towering green pines known as the "Trees of Faith." In 1934, as the Red Army embarked on the Long March, 17 young men from Huawu Village bid farewell to their families. Before departing, they planted these pine saplings on the mountainside, fully aware

that joining the revolution might cost them their lives. The trees they planted became a testament to their unwavering conviction: "As long as the green pines stand, the revolution will triumph!" Tragically, none of the 17 heroes returned from the northern expeditions—all became martyrs. Yet their spirit lives on, immortalized by the evergreen pines that stand sentinel over the land, their legacy etched into eternity.

如今,短短10年时间,华屋村从一个贫困落后的小山村,蝶变为"苏区振兴样板村""脱贫攻坚示范村""红色文化旅游特色村"……华屋的沧桑巨变,也是近10年来红都瑞金发展的真实写照。在实现全面小康、巩固脱贫攻坚成果、推进乡村振兴新征程中,瑞金人民承志奋进,着力书写着"处处皆华屋"的时代篇章。

In just a decade, Village Huawu has transformed from a poverty-stricken hamlet into a "Model Village for Soviet Area Revitalization" a "Poverty Alleviation Demonstration Village," and a "Red Culture Tourism Village." This extraordinary metamorphosis mirrors the broader development of Ruijin, the "Red Capital," over the past ten years. As Ruijin strides toward comprehensive prosperity, consolidates poverty eradication achievements, and advances rural revitalization, its people carry forward the revolutionary legacy, forging a new chapter where "every corner resonates with the spirit of Huawu."

时代画卷
Scroll of the Era

改革发展日新月异，幸福指数出圈出彩

Reform and Development are Changing with Each Passing Day, and the Happiness Index is out of the Ordinary

在大数据与AI算法交织的虚拟视野里，DeepSeek捕捉到南昌独特的城市魅力，它从历史深处走来，在现代浪潮中蓬勃发展，以独特的城市气质吸引着外地人、本地人，成为互联网时代的现象级网红城市。南昌已经成为外地人眼中的文化长廊，本地人的精神原乡。

In the digital landscape where big data converges with AI algorithms, DeepSeek's analytical prowess unveils Nanchang's multifaceted urban allure—a city emerging from

historical legacy while thriving as a booming metropolis. With its unique urban style, Nanchang has attrated outsiders and locals, cementing its status as China's latest viral urban phenomenon. To outsiders, Nanchang unfolds as an immersive cultural tapestry; to residents, it remains an unshakable spiritual anchor.

旅游"特种兵"

"Travel Warriors"

南昌地铁站内行李"排长龙"?这道"风景线"太暖心。原来,来南昌游玩的旅游"特种兵"太多,各大地铁站点提供免费行李寄存服务,民警、辅警"保姆式"看护。这一幕让不少网友直呼"上大分"。

A heartwarming "luggage queue" has become a unique sight in Nanchang's metro stations. The scene unfolds as travelers dubbed "tourism commandos" for their intensive sightseeing trips flood into the city, prompting metro stations system-wide to offer free luggage storage services. Police officers and auxiliary staff provide attentive oversight of the belongings, creating what netizens have hailed as a "model service worth applauding".

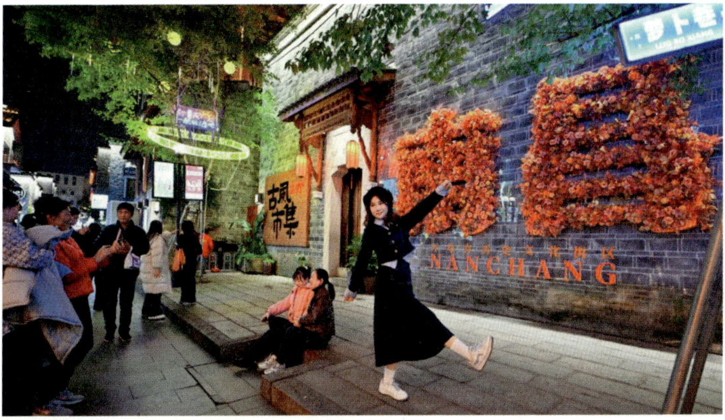
萝卜巷
NANCHANG

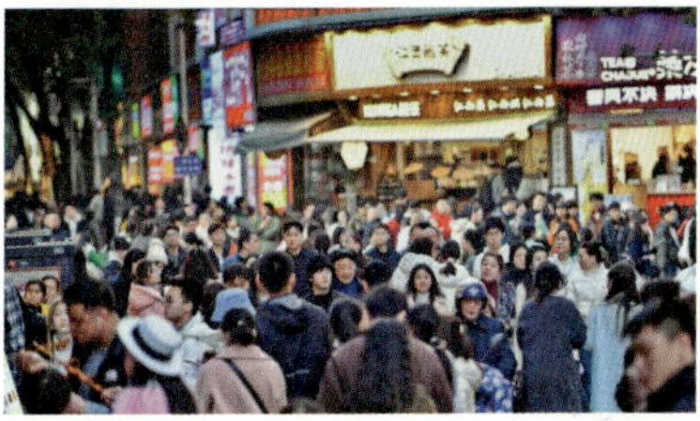

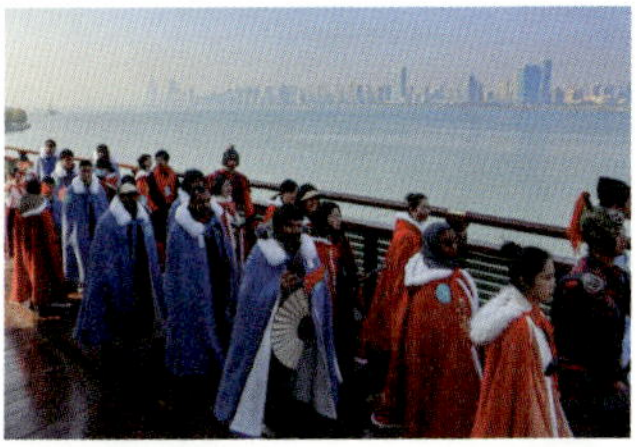

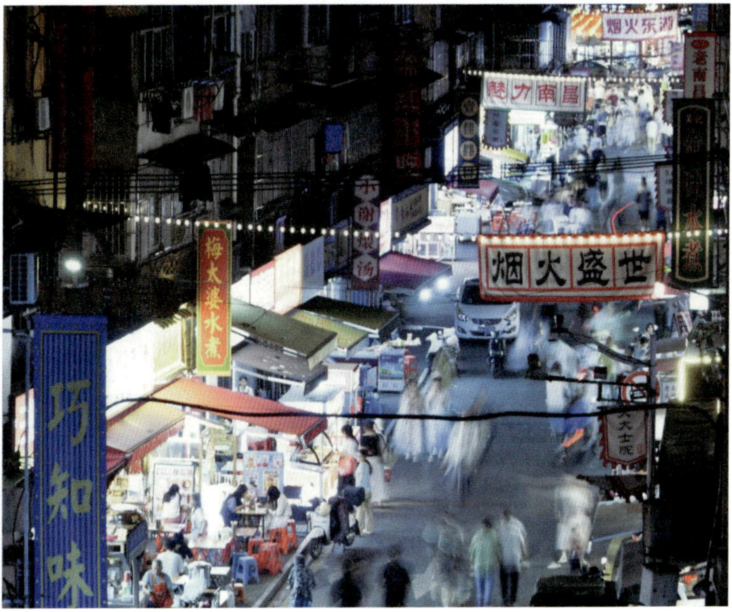
烟火东湖
魅力南昌
烟火盛世
梅太婆水煮
巧知味

烟花秀

Fireworks Show

2025年1月29日晚，农历正月初一，以"豫章春色　人间烟火"为主题的南昌迎春烟花晚会在赣江之心"老官洲"水域举行。晚会时长40分钟，采用"船上+楼上"的燃放模式，布置多条烟花船只，形成长达1300米的烟花阵地，璀璨烟花在赣江之畔的滕王阁上空绽放，吸引了数十万中外游客现场观礼。烟花秀也成为

南昌节庆的常规节目。

On the evening of January 29, 2025 (the first day of the first lunar month), Nanchang's Spring Festival Gala Fireworks Show, themed "Yuzhang's Spring Splendor: A Glimpse of Earthly Delights," illuminated the waters of "Laoguanzhou" in the heart of the Gan River. Lasting 40 minutes, the spectacle employed a dual-platform launch system combining "barge-mounted and land-based" pyrotechnics, with a 1,300-meter-long display line formed by multiple firework vessels. Dazzling bursts of light erupted above the historic Tengwang Pavilion along the riverbanks, captivating hundreds of thousands of domestic and international spectators who gathered to witness this luminous celebration. The event has since become a recurring highlight in Nanchang's festive calendar.

马拉松

Marathon

　　南昌，蓄势起跑的"马拉松之城"。3.5万名跑友在英雄城独特的一江两岸赛道上演绎了一场燃情的"万马奔腾"。这场声势浩大的"英雄马"，展现了天下英雄城"自信、发奋、齐心"的精气神，这是一座现代化都市在潮流奔涌中焕发出的激情与力量。要想认识一座城市，深入这座城市的生活，跑步是最好的方式之一。南昌城市马拉松，如今已成为流量经济中的大IP。

Nanchang has emerged as a thriving "Marathon City," where 35,000 runners converged on the unique "Riverside Symphony" course that winds through the City of Heroes, creating a roaring spectacle of collective energy. This grand-scale "Hero Marathon" embodies the spirit of Nanchang—confident, industrious, and united—showcasing the vitality and dynamism of a modern metropolis riding the tides of progress. For those seeking to truly understand a city and immerse themselves in its rhythm, running offers one of the most authentic experiences. Today, the Nanchang Urban Marathon stands as a major cultural IP in the era of attention economy.

鱼水情

Harmonious Relationship and Close Affinity

　　中华人民共和国75周年华诞，一场庄重热烈的升旗仪式在南昌八一广场隆重举行。护旗手在首，仪仗队居后，踏着铿锵有力的整齐步伐走来。伴随着雄壮激昂的《义勇军进行曲》，五星红旗冉冉升起，随风飘扬。现场数千军民肃立瞩目，齐唱国歌，穿着军绿 T 恤的一个萌娃，自发向仪仗队士兵敬礼。这一幕在网络上传播后立即出圈，成为军民鱼水情深的见证。

On the 75th anniversary of the People's Republic of China, a grand flag-raising ceremony was held at Nanchang's Bayi Square(八一广场), radiating solemnity and patriotic fervor. The flag-bearers led the procession, followed by the honor guard marching in precise, resolute steps that echoed like historical proclamations. As the stirring notes of the "March of the Volunteers" swelled, the national flag rose steadily, fluttering majestically against the dawn sky. Thousands of military personnel and civilians stood at solemn attention, their voices merging in the national anthem. Among them, an adorable toddler in a military-green T-shirt spontaneously saluted the soldiers—a moment that went viral instantly, embodying the profound bond between the military and civilians forged through decades of shared struggles and triumphs.

幸福食堂

Happy Canteen

　　老有所养，是千家万户的"心上事"，也是政府部门的"上心事"。宜春市袁州区湛郎街道五六川社区幸福食堂，老人们在食堂里愉快地用餐。袁州区综合考虑辖区老年人口规模、就餐需求、服务半径等因素，按照"一刻钟"就餐服务圈合理布局，建成20余家社区幸福食堂，让广大老年人在家门口就能吃上热乎乎的饭菜。同时，该区还充分发挥社区社会组织、党员志愿服务队作用，为行动不便的老人提供免费上门送餐服务，让老年人吃饭不再是难题，受到群众欢迎。

Ensuring the well-being of the elderly is a top priority for both households and government authorities. At the Wuliuchuan Community Happy Canteen in Zhanlang Subdistrict, Yuanzhou District, Yichun City, senior citizens enjoy their meals in a cheerful atmosphere. Taking into account factors such as the elderly population size, dining needs, and service coverage, Yuanzhou District has strategically established over 20 Happy Canteen in the community within a 15-minute meal service radius, enabling seniors to access hot meals right at their doorstep. Furthermore, the district leverages community organizations and volunteer teams composed of Party members to provide free meal delivery services for mobility-impaired elderly residents, effectively addressing dining challenges and earning widespread public approval.

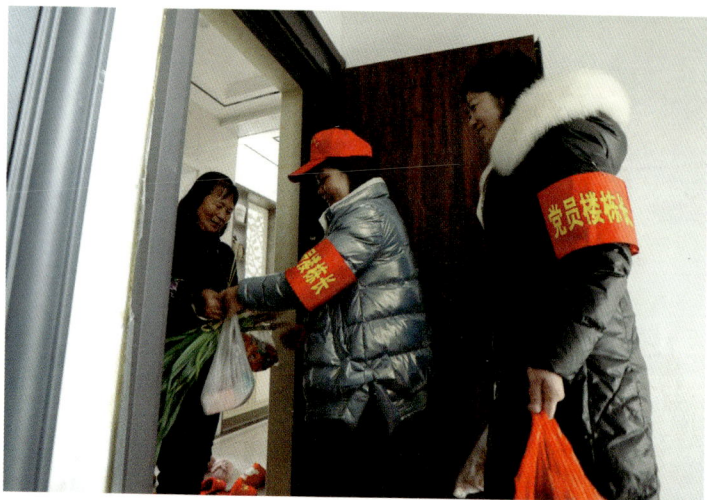

民生是人民幸福之基、社会和谐之本。一个个新的变化、一组组亮丽的数据见证了江西亮丽的"民生账单"，充分体现了江西始终"以百姓心为心"的不变初心。

Livelihood forms the cornerstone of happiness for the people and the foundation of social harmony. A series of changes and impressive statistical milestones attest to Jiangxi's remarkable performance in improving people's livelihood, underscoring its unwavering commitment to "prioritizing the people's well-being as its own"—a principle that has guided its governance from the very beginning.

数据显示，2024年江西城镇、农村居民人均可支配收入分别增长 4.3%、6.2%左右。年初确定的10件民生实事全部兑现，解决了一批群众急难愁盼问题。

Data shows that Jiangxi witnessed per capita disposable income growth of approximately 4.3% for urban residents and 6.2% for rural residents in 2024. All ten livelihood initiatives pledged at the beginning of the year have been fully realized, addressing a range of pressing issues affecting the public.

城乡低保、特困人员供养标准连续18年提高，城乡居民养老保险待遇水平稳居中部地区第一，折射出江西把更多的发展红利体现到老百姓的获得感上，也充分彰显了江西的"幸福底色"。

Subsistence allowances for urban and rural residents and support standards for individuals in extreme difficulty have been raised for 18 consecutive years, while pension benefits for urban and rural residents remain the highest in central China. These achievements reflect Jiangxi's commitment to ensuring development gains directly enhance the people's sense of fulfillment and happiness.

2025年，江西省政府工作报告绘就出了一幅更加锦绣的"民生图景"。

强化就业优先政策，用好"5+2就业之家"，做好高校毕业生、农民工、退役军人、脱贫劳动力等重点群体就业工作；

In 2025, Jiangxi's government work report has painted an even more vibrant "livelihood blueprint".

Strengthening the employment-first policy by leveraging the "5 + 2 Employment Home" to support key groups including college graduates, migrant workers, veterans, and formerly impoverished rural residents.

建设改造90家区域性中心敬老院,推动乡镇敬老院转型升级,建设300个"一老一小幸福院",提升老年助餐服务水平;

Constructing and renovating 90 regional central nursing homes, driving the transformation of township-level elderly care facilities, establishing 300 "happiness centers for seniors and children," and enhancing meal-delivery services for the elderly;

推动优质医疗资源扩容下沉,90%的县达到紧密型县域医共体标准,90%以上的村(社区)配备家庭健康指导员……

Expanding access to quality medical resources, ensuring 90% of counties meet standards for integrated county-level medical communities, and deploying family health advisors to over 90% of villages and communities...

可以看到,江西始终盯紧民生"小事""难事",以人民幸福生活为"指南针",做好民生"综合题",努力写好顺应群众期盼、增进民生福祉的"幸福答卷"。

红色基因代代传的奥秘,就是"以人民为中心"的执政理念落到了实处,赢得了人民的认同与拥护。

Jiangxi consistently prioritizes addressing both everyday challenges and persistent issues affecting people's lives. By anchoring its work in the pursuit of public well-being and taking a holistic approach to livelihood improvements, the province is actively composing a "happiness answer sheet" that aligns with the aspirations of its people and advances their welfare.

The secret to the red genes being passed down from generation to generation lies in the people-centered governance philosophy that having been put into practice and won the people's recognition and endorsement.

后　记

Afterword

　　《何以江西2024》是由江西省人民政府新闻办公室编写的省情读本，省委宣传部对外传播处负责编写出版组织工作。文本撰写由省委党校常务副校长李能、副校长高莉娟领衔，郭金丰、曾光、高建设、廖太燕、李林峰、花晨、杨和平、余漫负责完成，形成征求意见稿。江西日报社国际传播中心主任何宝庆领衔，毛江凡、洪怀峰、叶景顺、曾悦之、谢龙龙、毛萍等组成项目组，对全书从内容到形式进行整体优化，形成定稿。江西人民出版社组建了由社长总编辑、分管副社长、首席编辑、艺术总监、英文编辑构成的工作专班，提供全方位的编撰和出版服务。江西人民出版社组建了由社长总编辑、分管副社长、首席编辑、艺术总监构成的工作专班，提供全方位的出版服务。本书图片由江西日报社视觉中心、视觉江西、江西画报社等单位提供。

　　Jiangxi Before Jiangxi 2024 is a provincial situation reading book compiled by the Information Office of Jiangxi Provincial People's Government. The International Communication Office of the Publicity Department of Jiangxi Provincial Commitee is responsible for the publication. The text writing was led by Li Neng, Execution President of the Party School of Jiangxi Provincial Committee, and Gao Lijuan, Vice President. Guo Jinfeng, Zeng Guang, Gao Jianshe, Liao Taiyan, Li Linfeng, Hua Chen, Yang Heping, and Yu Man were responsible for completing the draft and soliciting opinions. Led by He Baoqing, Director of the International Communication Center of Jiangxi Daily Press, a project team consisted of Mao Jiangfan, Hong Huaifeng, Ye Jingshun, Zeng Yuezhi, Xie Longlong, and Mao Ping, conducted a comprehensive optimization of the book from content to form, resulting in the final draft. Jiangxi People's Publishing House established a specialized team consisted of the President and Editor-in-Chief, Vice Presidents in Charge, the Chief Editor, and the Artistic Director to provide comprehensive publishing services. The pictures are provided by the Visual Center of Jiangxi Daily, Vision Jiangxi, and Jiangxi Pictorial, etc.

　　本书编写过程中，还得到了省政府办公厅、省发展和改革委、省科技厅、省工业和信息化厅、省人力资源和社会保障厅、省自然资源厅、省生态环境厅、省农业农村厅、省商务厅、省文化和旅游厅、省外办、省统计局等单位的大力支持。对此，我们表示衷心感谢！

　　The compilation of this book has received strong support from General Office of Jiangxi Provincial People's Government and Jiangxi Provincial Development and Reform Commission, Department of Science and Technology of Jiangxi Province, Jiangxi Provincial Department of Industry and Information Technology, Department of Human Resources and Social Security of Jiangxi Province, Department of Natural Resources of Jiangxi Province, Department of Ecology and Environment of Jiangxi Province, Department of Agriculture and Rural Affairs of Jiangxi Province, Department of Commerce of Jiangxi Province, Department of Culture and Tourism of Jiangxi Province, Foreign Affairs Office of Jiangxi Provincial People's Government, and Jiangxi Provincial Statistics Bureau, etc. We express our heartfelt gratitude for their support!

编写组（Writing Group）

2025年5月（May 2025）

摄影(按姓氏音序排列):

艾世民　陈良帅　陈声年　陈思伟　邓和平　丁铭华

段长征　冯 尧　高科峰　郭廷良　海 波　韩俊烜

洪子波　李方图　李建平　李剑涛　李 劼　李 敏

李小明　梁振堂　廖 敏　林朝晖　刘佳惠子　刘芸池

马 刚　宁秀云　邱业成　裴莎莎　阮 琼　史港泽

宋靖辉　田 野　田友锋　涂星星　涂序理　王国红

王和耀　王建旭　王 祺　王 强　魏东升　吴福清

吴文兵　肖南波　肖 英　谢凌阳　熊思炜　熊薇薇

徐国亮　徐 铮　许安萍　许南平　杨继红　叶 波

印德智　袁建兵　袁 骏　袁 云　张翰林　张 龙

钟万汕　周 桐　朱定文　朱海鹏　朱文标　卓忠伟

邹 俊　邹宇波

Photographers(arranged alphabetically by surname):

Ai Shimin, Chen Liangshuai, Chen Shengnian, Chen Siwei, Deng Heping, Ding Minghua, Duan Changzheng, Feng Yao, Gao Kefeng, Guo Tingliang, Hai Bo, Han Junxuan, Hong Zibo, Li Fangtu, Li Jianping, Li Jiantao, Li Jie, Li Min, Li Xiaoming, Liang Zhentang, Liao Min, Lin Zhaohui, Liu Jiahuizi, Liu Yunchi, Ma Gang, Ning Xiuyun, Qiu Yecheng, Qiu Shasha, Ruan Qiong, Shi Gangze, Song Jinghui, Tian Ye, Tian Youfeng, Tu Xingxing, Tu Xuli, Wang Guohong, Wang Heyao, Wang Jianxu, Wang Qi, Wang Qiang, Wei Dongsheng, Wu Fuqing, Wu Wenbing, Xiao Nanbo, Xiao Ying, Xie Lingyang, Xiong Siwei, Xiong Weiwei, Xu Guoliang, Xu Zheng, Xu Anping, Xu Nanping, Yang Jihong, Ye Bo, Yin Dezhi, Yuan Jianbing, Yuan Jun, Yuan Yun, Zhang Hanlin, Zhang Long, Zhong Wanshan, Zhou Tong, Zhu Dingwen, Zhu Haipeng, Zhu Wenbiao, Zhuo Zhongwei, Zou Jun, Zou Yubo

感谢李小明、邓和平等一众摄友。个别图片因未能联系到作者,请及时与江西人民出版社联系(jxpph@tom.com),在此一并表示感谢!

We express our gratitude to Li Xiaoming, Deng Heping, and other photography enthusiasts. Some of the photos were unable to be attributed to their photographers.Please contact Jiangxi People's Publishing House promptly (jxpph@tom.com),and we extend our gratitude here as well!